Like a Mask
Dancing
A Tanzanian Story

Illustration by Vonnie Whitworth

Like a Mask Dancing

A Tanzanian Story

Sally Stiles

Pale Horse Books

Library of Congress # 2020900046

ISBN 978-1-9399-03-4

Other books by Sally Stiles
available through Pale Horse Books,
Barnes & Noble
and Amazon.com:

Plunge! A Memoir
Crazeman in the Bottle
Haiku Guide to the Inside Passage
The Haiku Guide to Williamsburg
The Haiku Guide to Cruising (the Pacific Northwest)

Cover and frontispiece illustrations by Vonnie Whitworth.
Author photo by Lisa W. Cumming.

"The world is like a mask dancing.
If you want to see it well,
you do not stand in one place."

Chinua Achebe
Arrow of God

"A stone, a leaf, an unfound door....
Which of us has known his brother....
Which of us is not forever a stranger
and alone?"

Thomas Wolfe
Look Homeward, Angel

Again, because of David

"Thy people shall be my people…"

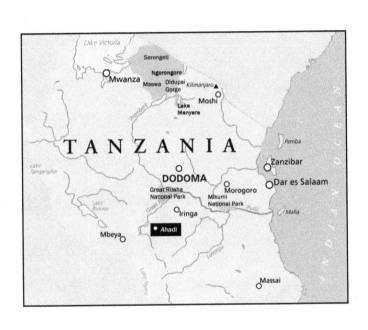

A Tanzanian Story

PART ONE

Karibu
Welcome

March 1990

CHAPTER ONE: THE LONE WREN

*A*nna Chadwick was not the first woman to follow a man to Africa. There had been many before her, some of whom fled back to their more comfortable homelands, while others settled in and thrived.

Over twenty-four years of marriage, Anna had joined her husband, Aaron, senior vice-president of Transnational Development, on a half-dozen business trips abroad. While in Europe, Asia and Indonesia, she'd glimpsed cultures distinctive from her own, but those trips had been brief, too brief to provide her with more than a cursory understanding of what she'd observed. She wondered if, as a resident of Tanzania for a year or so, she would remain a stranger, an observer rather than a participant.

She imagined herself a wren hovering just outside a flock of kingfishers, and, while she laughed at the image, she knew there was something to it: she, the lone wren, standing on the sidelines while her husband became leader of the flock.

A Tanzanian Story

She loved Aaron, treasured her marriage and wanted to fall asleep each night and awaken each morning at his side. But even on this, her first day in the coastal city of Dar Es Salaam, amid the cacophony of bright colors, mixed languages, tempos, scents, she knew she wouldn't thrive on love alone. She would need to find a way to travel with the flock.

When they'd arrived at Dar Es Salaam's Julius Nyerere airport mid-morning, after three days of travel from Vermont, they'd stepped outside the terminal to be met by oppressive heat and by Jabari Tamin, a company driver. He'd loaded their two large suitcases into the boot of a blue Land Cruiser and steered them through the burgeoning city to the Oyster Bay Executive Inn. They'd climbed up to their second-floor room, stepped over their unopened suitcases, turned up the air-conditioning and flopped onto the thin mattress. Anna awoke two hours later having dreamt of wandering through a mansion, each vibrantly painted corridor a dead end, each room tightly sealed.

After dinner, they met Eric and Glenna Sikes in the lobby bar. Aaron was replacing Eric as general manager of Tanzania's largest industrial project, the paper mill in Ahadi, some 800 kilometers west of Dar Es Salaam, a village Anna couldn't find on any of her maps of Tanzania.

Eric, his cinnamon-brown hair thinning under a comb-over, his mustache stubbly and beard rough, had held middle management posts on projects Aaron reviewed in Algeria and Thailand, but tonight it was as if they'd never met. Eric's hazel eyes were dull, impassive, and he avoided looking at either Aaron or Anna. He evaded Aaron's questions about production, personnel, funding. "That mill will never be profitable," he said and shrugged his shoulders when Aaron asked him why.

But Glenna Sikes, his petite and slender, considerably younger second wife, with a striking olive complexion, silky long black hair and flashing eyes, made up for his reticence. She talked about the beautiful view from their house at the top of the hill in Ahadi, about the large garden and Tobias, so helpful in the kitchen and the garden, too. "He really ought to be working as a hotel chef," she said. "He's that good."

Suddenly she turned and aimed a sharp-shooter squint at Anna. "Keep the storeroom in the house stocked with food and locked."

Before Anna had a chance to respond, Glenna switched the topic. "Ryder McGowan's wife—what was her name?" She raised an eyebrow toward Eric.

"Bella," Eric mumbled.

"Oh yes, well, she only stayed a couple of weeks, then high-tailed it back to the U.K. Couldn't take it. Bella told me she fed her help on banana leaves, no utensils. She said they're used to eating with their hands, and she didn't want their germs on her good dishes. Can you imagine?"

Eric rolled his eyes toward the ceiling.

Glenna continued. "And what's her name, Bella, she wouldn't let her houseboy make bread after she saw him with his hands in the dough." She took a quick swallow of her drink. "How else are you going to knead the dough? My boy, Tobias, makes wonderful bread. Cakes, too. He really could be a chef."

Glenna took a deep breath, sighed, turned to look out the window. "I am so ready to go home."

"Glenna," Eric said, "Drink up. I think it's time—"

She waved her hand toward him and, in the process, knocked over his whiskey glass. Without hesitating, she called to the waiter for a refill.

As the waiter bent low to wipe up the scotch, Glenna squinted again at Anna. "I hope you take good care of that garden. It nearly crushed my soul to leave it for thieves to destroy." She sighed again and repeated herself: "I am so ready to go home."

Anna shrunk down into her seat, having no idea how to reply. She couldn't sort out what was true and what was hyperbole. She only knew that she still had much to learn about Africa, about Tanzania, and everything to learn about a village called Ahadi.

Aaron cut the meeting short, slapped a stack of shilling notes down on the table, grabbed Anna's hand and led her from the bar. After they rounded the corner, he stopped by the stairs leading up to their room. "I have a feeling the mill may be in more trouble than I realized," he said. "I just hope it's salvageable."

"I know you well enough," Anna said, "to know that the rescue squad is on its way."

He grinned, tousled her curly blonde hair, cut short just before they left home, and they continued up the stairs.

§§§

The next morning, a Sunday, Anna opened the window of her room at the hotel to steam rising from the pavement and an acrid odor—sea salt mixed with wood smoke, along with a heavy, sour smell, like the stench of rotting vegetation. She reached for her camera, a new Canon EOS 1, attached the motor drive and put the setting on autofocus.

Below her, Glenna Sikes slipped across the parking lot, heading toward the Land Cruiser. She wore white high-heel sandals, a black and white striped sundress, and a white cardigan dangled from the turquoise tote bag slung across her

12

shoulder. In her wake, a porter struggled to push a luggage cart wobbling under four scuffed-up suitcases, two hanging bags and three heavily taped cardboard boxes.

Through the viewfinder, Anna watched the desk clerk dart past Glenna, balancing on his head an outsized Samsonite suitcase, turquoise like the tote bag, its little wheels spinning in the air. *Zoom in, click, whirr.*

Next, Aaron emerged from the hotel. He smoothed back the mop of honey-brown hair which tended to spill across his forehead. His long legs cast an even longer shadow behind him. *Zoom out, click, whirr.*

When Aaron approached Glenna, she dropped her tote bag and turned to join her husband standing at the edge of the driveway and smoking a cigar. Eric, his head high, was looking out toward the street as if he played no part in the scene taking place behind him.

Glenna took the cigar from his mouth, kissed him, then whispered in his ear before leading him back to the hotel. They stood in the shade of the portico while the driver loaded the car.

As Aaron watched the scene unfold, his mouth curled up into a half smile. He walked to the back of the Land Cruiser to help Jabari load the luggage.

Jabari was solidly built and only a few inches taller than Anna's five foot six. His rounded nose, sculptured cheekbones and russet coloring reminded her of Rubens' *Four Studies of a Moor.* She knelt and held her camera steady on the windowsill to capture him in profile: *zoom in, click, whirr, click, whirr.*

Jabari took the third box from Aaron, shoved it into the boot of the Land Cruiser, then removed his Kufi skullcap and retrieved a handkerchief from his pocket, first wiping

13

the sweat from his brow, then from the back of his neck. He stuffed the handkerchief back in his pocket and eyed the large turquoise suitcase. He measured it with his hands, then, again using his hands, measured the space left in the back of the Land Cruiser, hefted the suitcase and tossed it sideways onto the floor of the front passenger seat, then tossed the tote bag on top of it. Glenna's white sweater fell to the ground. He shook it out and carefully laid it on top of the tote bag.

Anna closed the window, placed her camera on the ledge and sat, head thrown back against the stiff upholstery of the chair beside the bed. In her mind she reviewed the photos she had just taken, pausing at the picture of Aaron leading his long shadow across the pavement, then again at Jabari, beads of sweat across his broad brow. And then she began to reminisce back to an earlier time, a time when she had yet to discover who she might be and how she might truly love the man she had married.

CHAPTER TWO: OLD SCARS

Soon after the birth of their son, Christopher, Anna and Aaron Chadwick retreated from their small apartment in New York City to a three-bedroom house in Connecticut. As Christopher grew, Anna gravitated toward predictable but unrewarding commitments to the PTA and the Junior League. While she played tennis, took yoga and watercolor classes and served on the library board, she felt she was just dabbling. She longed for work, meaningful work, such as the research job she'd held at the Metropolitan Museum before they'd moved from the city. When Christopher was older and needed his mother less, Anna grew more discontented.

All those years, Aaron commuted to the city and was promoted from assistant manager to manager to vice president, and, finally, to senior vice president of development and oversight for Transnational Development. The company owned or operated industrial projects world-wide, primarily chemical plants, packaging companies and pulp and paper mills. He would leave home for weeks at a time, sometimes circling the globe, often landing at sites with no reliable telephone service. Even when he was back working at his office in the Chrysler Building, he seldom left the city in time to catch the express commuter train. He often stayed late or overnight in Manhattan to entertain clients or catch up on work—or so he said.

Anna forced herself to believe him, yet she felt a tacit tension growing between them. She began to question where he'd been and who he was with. He grew more defensive,

15

then more elusive.

Aaron returned from a trip to Kuala Lumpur with two bottles of duty-free Joy perfume in his suitcase. He gave her the larger one and told her the smaller one was for Carina Sorenstam, his assistant. At first, Anna thought he was being considerate.

A month later, Anna and Aaron were on the tarmac in Minneapolis, stowing bags under their seats in a corporate jet which would fly them up to the 700-acre 3M retreat in Northern Minnesota. Along with some twenty other executives, most of them accompanied by their wives, they were the guests of 3M's industrial sales department for a weekend of cross-country skiing, snowmobiling, ice fishing and relaxing by the large stone fireplace in the lodge.

Anna had just settled into her seat on the plane when Carina Sorenstam walked down the aisle, her ice blue eyes glistening. She wore a sleek black ski jumpsuit and greeted them with a smile that seemed to Anna to include the hint of a smirk. Before Carina slipped into the seat across from Aaron, she leaned down toward him. Her long blonde hair brushed his shoulder. "This sure beats the coach-class squeeze on the trip to Golden last week," she said.

Aaron nodded at her but didn't respond. Instead, he looked quickly at Anna, as if checking her reaction. Anna breathed in deeply, catching a whiff of Joy perfume.

As soon as they entered their room at the stylishly rustic Pineview lodge, Anna wanted to ask Aaron point-blank if he was having an affair. But she backed off. She went to the window and opened the curtains. Their room overlooked Big Mantrap Lake, ice glistening under a dusting of snow. "Did you go skiing while you were in Colorado?"

"Of course not, Anna. Remember I was gone all of two

and a half days, and a lot of that time was spent at 40,000 feet in the air."

"Why is Carina here?"

"Come on, Anna." Aaron sighed before responding in a hard-edged tone. "When Howard Hammond couldn't come at the last minute, he suggested Carina take his place. He said it would be good for people to begin to know her as a part of our team."

Anna finally turned to face him. He was sitting on the end of the bed, his eyes lowered, fists clenched. "But I thought she was like a secretary," Anna said.

He unclenched his hands and rubbed the back of his neck before looking up at Anna. "She's an administrative assistant. All the women we've ever hired are telephone operators, typists or, if they have a business degree, like Carina, they might be a departmental administrator or assistant. She's worked for us for two years, lately with a lot of overtime because of my too-many projects. She's familiar with most of the jobs I'm working on, and if she's willing to take on more responsibility, I'd like to see her promoted to cover more of my workload."

"You're telling me that Transnational is actually beginning to welcome women into the corporate ranks? Are you finally becoming a feminist?"

"Hey, it's not my fault that Yale didn't admit women until after I graduated," he said, flashing a quick grin. "And I think your alma mater still excludes men."

"Touché," she said.

Aaron's tone softened. "The time is long past due to promote women," he said. "In this case, however, I believe that Carina is more than casually attracted to Howard Hammond. The feeling may be mutual."

"Howard Hammond is twice her age. And married," Anna said.

"Please, come sit down." Aaron patted the bed beside him. She didn't move.

"Anna, I have too much to lose by getting involved with someone else. And, in case you've forgotten, I once promised to forsake all others to marry you."

"I made the same promise, Aaron. And I meant what I said."

"Please. Let it go. If Carina can take over some of my projects, I might even get home on time more often."

"More often?" She couldn't remember the last time he was home before seven.

After dinner, while Aaron was in the bar, competing in a hotly-contested dart game, Anna said she was tired and returned to the room. She lay down on the bed and massaged the back of her neck, surprised at how much tension she had allowed to lodge between her shoulder blades.

She began to wonder what had happened that she could be suspicious of the man she thought she knew how to love, jealous of a woman colleague who was attractive, yes, flirtatious, yes, invested in Aaron's work, yes, all those things. But how many other women like her had Aaron known through the years? And hadn't she, just last week, openly flirted with her cousin's new boyfriend? The overworked husband; the bored housewife. Had their marriage become a cliché?

§§§

For her birthday that April, Aaron gave Anna a Leica R4, a professional-quality compact reflex camera. He included a 28mm wide-angle lens and a 90mm portrait lens. He also gave her an airline ticket to join him on an upcoming business trip to Japan. Christopher, now a high-school junior,

18

would spend the week with the Andrews family down the street. Their son, Tom, had been Christopher's best friend since second grade.

While Aaron was in meetings in Tokyo, Anna spent the hours with her new camera photographing the gardens and shrines. For half a day she wandered through the small Edo-period Mukojima-Hyakkaen garden. She photographed exuberant red blooms on the flowering quince, plum blossoms overhead, a brilliant blue passionflower clinging to a vine. She walked back and forth through the lattice arbors, one dripping in heavy clusters of wisteria, emitting a musky scent.

She crossed and re-crossed the bridges over the long pond and photographed the reflection of plants in the dense water—every shape conceivable, every shade of green, a splash of pink from an overhead branch loaded with cherry blossoms. With her camera, she followed the fluttering wings of a dragonfly. She photographed the poems posted throughout the garden, having no idea what the hiragana characters meant, but admiring the elegant calligraphy.

Here she felt apart from the city, from the passersby, some who bowed, all who went on their way without speaking. It was as if her camera were inviting her to examine more closely, to appreciate more fully, all she observed.

As she left the bamboo gate, she picked up a brochure and, on the way back to the hotel, read that in March of 1944 the garden had been annihilated when the US Army Air Force firebombed Tokyo. Much was demolished—plum trees, iris, poetry, the pupae of emerging dragonflies. And yet, 40 years later, the garden bloomed again to provide city dwellers a small preserve, a sanctuary in the heart of the metropolis.

On the weekend, they traveled to Kyoto and stayed at

the Hiragiya Ryokan where they soaked in a tub overlooking a garden of moss, decorative stones and lanterns. They drank warm sake, dined privately at a low table in their room and made love on a futon unfurled across the tatami floor.

The next day they explored the Daitoku-ji Temple where, again, Anna felt a compelling curiosity about what she saw through her Leica lens. She went through two rolls of film photographing the flowers, the curved oversized roofs, the decorative tiles. She took pictures of the monks strolling by, and the raked gravel garden—a long expanse of perfect circles, swirls and stripes, not a pebble out of place. She was so absorbed by what she was seeing through the lens that she was startled when Aaron touched her elbow and said: "We really should leave. There's more to see in Kyoto."

"Just one more picture," she said. And ten minutes later, "Just one more."

When they returned home, Anna enrolled in a summer semester class at the School of Visual Arts in the city. She learned about shutter speeds, lighting, exposure, filters, composition. She studied the images displayed in galleries and museums, read books about photography, took pictures nearly every day. She and Aaron spent a weekend setting up a darkroom in their basement. She enrolled in more classes, and Aaron cheered her on. Late the next July, he helped her set up a booth at the Old Saybrook arts festival where she sold her first images and won the best in photography award for her silhouetted portrait of a Kyoto monk.

Sunday night after the festival closed, they had just or- dered dinner in a restaurant overlooking the sound when Aaron took a long gulp of his scotch, laid the glass on the table and cleared his throat. "I'm tired," he said, "of packing and unpacking my suitcase."

He told Anna he wanted to run a business Transnational was negotiating to acquire, a failing papermill in Vermont. He gazed toward the cove where the Connecticut River emptied into the sound. "I just want to spend evenings on my back deck, listening to the perpetual flow of that river. I want to drive to work along curved roads where cows graze on the hillsides. And I want to save the jobs of a hundred long-time, loyal employees."

"Aaron, how long have you been thinking about this?"

He laughed. "I'll admit I've been keeping an eye on the place for a couple of years. Remember I told you I stopped by the mill on my way back from Quebec? It looked like a promising acquisition for Transnational. It's an older mill, but the machinery's been well maintained. There's a new winder and an even newer sheeter. Experienced employees. But the management is floundering. Howard Hammond has agreed, so he and I will be going up next week—hopefully to close the deal. You should come along."

"I'm ready," Anna said. Aaron would be home each night. Christopher would be a freshman at Dartmouth College, only half an hour away. Maybe they'd be a family again. The river, the mountains, the meadows: she would have new landscapes to photograph. Yes, the move to Vermont could be exactly what they needed to seal the nearly mended fissure between them.

As they lay in bed at the Old Saybrook Inn that night, Aaron took Margaret Atwood's *The Handmaid's Tale* from Anna's hands, turned off the light and wrapped his legs across hers. "I hope—how I hope—," he whispered, "that they will let me take this job. I've spent too many nights in too many dismal hotel rooms missing you. I don't want to lose the remarkable woman I married."

§§§

Within a year, the Vermont mill was meeting production goals. Anna was getting her photographs placed in art galleries in Vermont and New Hampshire. She'd nabbed two assignments for *Upper Valley Magazine*, one for *Yankee*, and joined the faculty at Lebanon College where she taught photography classes. A gallery in Boston picked up half a dozen of her newest landscapes. She was beginning to feel optimistic about her emerging career.

She and Aaron spent more time together than they had in many years. They skied on winter weekends, canoed the river and nearby lakes in the summer and developed a small circle of creative and well-traveled friends. The scratch in their love had healed. Neither of them were looking for old scars.

§§§

Four years after their move to Vermont, Aaron, at age forty-nine, felt he had more significant work ahead of him. Eric Sikes' term was ending, and the Tanzanian Minister of Industries told Transnational Development they must come up with a highly qualified replacement if they wanted to retain the management contract. So, Aaron, eager to create a future for a troubled paper mill built to bolster the economy of an impoverished East African nation, volunteered for the job.

"Anna," he said, "Tanzania is an extraordinary country of mountains and forests and game preserves. The people are welcoming, peace-loving. I've seen pictures of the townsite, and the general manager's house sits on top of the hill overlooking a valley. There's a large garden. And a gardener. If you'll come with me, I think we're in store for a great adventure."

She shook her head. "We're happy here."

"I won't go without you. But if I don't take this job, I have a feeling I'll be back in the home office before too long."

After a restless week of anxiety, Anna said yes. She began to imagine the people she would meet, the faces and landscapes she would photograph. She went to Life Extension Institute in New York for a battery of inoculations and then, since she'd leave her treasured Leica at home, to Willoughby's to shop for a new camera.

§§§

A week later, Christopher was hugging them good-bye at the British Airways terminal in Boston before they boarded their first flight toward Dar Es Salaam.

Christopher had graduated from Dartmouth and was gaining experience by working for WVTA, the Windsor, Vermont PBS television station. He would live at the house and care for their eight-year old German Shepherd, Murray. Christopher appreciated the rent-free arrangement. Anna appreciated having him care for the house and Murray.

In the boarding area, Anna watched her son walk away from them, his shoulders hunched. He turned and waved, smiled like a brave warrior heading into battle, then continued down the concourse, smacking his fist against his palm—once, then again.

As they rose from their seats to join the line for boarding, Christopher ran back to them. "I forgot to tell you something," he said. "I love you, and you're welcome to come back." He hesitated and, with a wry smile, said, "Just not right away, but whenever you're ready."

They laughed and hugged each other again. Anna wiped a tear from Christopher's eye. He wiped one from hers. As the aircraft turned toward the runway, Christopher was watching from the window in the empty boarding area.

They flew overnight from Boston to London, went into the city for a stroll and fish and chips at the Grenadier Pub, then returned to the airport for a nap at the terminal hotel until boarding their late-night British Airways flight. As the sun rose, they were flying past Mount Kilimanjaro, an unbroken ring of clouds circling the flat, snow-draped summit, and 45 minutes later were skirting the Indian Ocean between the island of Zanzibar and the city of Dar Es Salaam. An hour and a half later they'd checked into their room at the Oyster Bay Executive Inn.

CHAPTER THREE: HAVEN OF PEACE

*L*ate morning on Sunday, the day after their arrival, Jabari returned from delivering the Sikes to the airport for the first leg of their journey back to Long Island. Aaron took the car keys, and he and Anna left the hotel to explore the city, founded by Sultan Sayyid Majid of Zanzibar as a fishing village in the 1860s. The name was derived from the Arabic, *House* or *Haven of Peace*.

Aaron hopped into the right-side driver's seat and appeared comfortable navigating from the left side of the road, though, for the first five miles, Anna felt uneasy in the left-side passenger seat. They drove through the central district with broad streets and multi-colored high-rise buildings, some freshly painted and some rust-stained, many with windows recessed behind railed balconies. Then they wound their way through back neighborhoods, drove down narrow streets filled with people darting in and out of ramshackle houses and shops. Bananas, mangos, melons and dried fish were displayed on rough wood tables, and American tee-shirts and *kangas*, the brightly colored strips of cloth women wore as skirts or wraps, swayed from awnings sagging over the stalls.

They passed an apparently empty structure pieced together from scraps of wood, cardboard and tin. Next to it was an open lot. Two boys, aged maybe six and eight, wearing torn shirts, no shoes, were kicking a ball of string between the garbage piles.

"Oh, Aaron, those children." He turned his head to watch the boys, then braked suddenly to avoid hitting a dog zig-zagging across the road. The brindled mongrel took a few steps forward then flopped down in the middle of a pothole to chew on his tail. He rose, turned around, moved a few feet forward and collapsed again.

Anna looked back at the boys, then at the dog, again at the boys. When the smaller boy stumbled into a garbage heap, the older one tried to pull him up by the armpits, but the little one fell back into the rubbish.

"Oh, my God!" she said. "Where are their parents?"

Aaron spun the wheel sharply left and accelerated around the dog. "I don't know," he said, "but it's possible those children may be living on their own."

"How can that be?"

"Many reasons," he said. "Maybe AIDS. The number of orphans from AIDS is mounting rapidly in Sub-Saharan Africa."

"But surely there are orphanages...churches...the government...something...."

"There are all those things," Aaron said, his voice husky. "But never enough. And I understand that, in most of Africa, there is still a good deal of misinformation, even denial of AIDS. Then there's the stigma attached." He shook his head. "Even at home."

One of Aaron's fraternity brothers had recently died of AIDS. Though there were many of his classmates living in the Boston area, Aaron was the only one to attend the funeral.

Anna turned in her seat. The dog was rolled over on his side in the middle of the road. The children were now out of sight. She thought of Christopher, when he was eight, and how ill-equipped he would have been to take care of himself, much less a younger brother. She imagined him wandering the neighborhood, begging for food. But wouldn't the Andrews down the street have taken him in, fed him, hopefully loved him nearly as much as she did?

"Aaron—those boys—isn't there something we can do?"

Aaron reached over and rubbed her knee. "Honey, I wish. I wish, but this isn't our country, our town. We would probably get in a heap of trouble if we tried to interfere."

Anna understood, but, still, she couldn't erase the images of the dog, of the two boys, from her mind. Once again, she felt helpless, an observer rather than a participant.

A few blocks farther on they passed an enclosed corporate enclave which looked like a miniature country club village with a swimming pool and tennis courts. Then they drove through a section of town where large, bright stucco homes were safeguarded by tall iron fences. From there they rattled down an unpaved road to the Bahari Beach Club which turned out to be a holiday oasis for the wealthy: round stone buildings and thatched roofs, swimming pools and white beaches overlooking the brilliant turquoise waters of the Indian Ocean. They got out of the car and walked toward the restaurant where lobster thermidor was one of several unexpected items on the menu posted outside.

Aaron often ordered lobster thermidor, but today he hunched his shoulders, turned from the restaurant and walked quickly away. She caught up with him and took his hand.

Down the road was the fish market, and they stopped to watch dhows skimming by. Boats slipped quickly past them, their sharp bows pointed into the wind. Some of the boats were no bigger than a canoe; others more like small sailing vessels. A few were tall with rough wood planks cribbing the stern. In the small dhow closest to shore, a fisherman grappled with the net while another wrestled with the sail. Anna reached into her shoulder bag for her camera and took a picture of their dark bodies straining against the sea.

Aaron's eyes never wavered from a boat headed out toward the vanishing point. She asked him what he was thinking.

"Hmm?" he asked. "What?"

He was still looking out at the sea when the boat disappeared over the horizon. "Just pondering," he said. He sniffed the air and smiled. "Kind of fishy around here, don't you think? Let's go."

Anna assumed he was pondering what he might find in Ahadi.

§§§

They returned to town via Haile Selassie Boulevard and parked at Oyster Bay. On the white sand beach were scores of people representing all the shades of humanity. Most of the young men wore American tee-shirts, and the young women, sitting two or three together, wore immaculate Western dresses and followed the boys with shy eyes.

Children climbed palm trees; toddlers somersaulted in the sand. Three Sikh women in long black burkas walked by slowly, accompanied by young men who appeared to be their older sons. An Indian boy, who looked to be about ten, raced his white pony through the surf, passed them, waved, turned and raced back. Anna photographed him at slow film speed to try to capture drops of water flying from the pony's hooves.

At five o'clock the food concessions appeared. A young, dark-skinned man wearing an orange and blue Hawaiian shirt set up a rusty oil drum and, when the fire began to flame, he placed a grate across the top and laid out tight rows of unhusked corn. A white-haired Indian assembled a charcoal grill and covered it with split, peeled cassava. To each serving he added a dollop of oil, a spoonful of chopped tomatoes and onions, and, as soon as the aroma seeped across the beach, people drifted toward him.

Anna's head was swimming in images, all brilliantly lit by the strong African sun which was finally sinking into the sea. She felt the weight of their long day of near-the-equator heat, the blend of wealth and poverty, mindless leisure and grueling work.

On the way back to the hotel, they stopped at an outdoor restaurant which appeared to occupy a vacant lot in Oyster Bay. All the food was prepared on a large grate and brought to the tables by waiters dripping sweat. The curried prawns were perfect—neither too soft nor too tough—and Aaron ordered a second helping of buttered garlic naan which they devoured as soon as it arrived, but Anna couldn't relax to enjoy the meal, couldn't dismiss what she'd seen that day: a country-club village, a pristine beach, a boy on a white pony, an emaciated hound, two boys in tatters kicking a ball of string through a garbage dump.

A Tanzanian Story

CHAPTER FOUR: THE LORD WILL PROVIDE

*M*id-day Monday, after Aaron returned from a brief introductory visit at the Ministry of Industries, they headed out of Dar es Salaam. Jabari drove on the sometimes paved, more often furrowed and dusty roads, chugged up hills and sped through sharp curves. To Anna, the country seemed immense, and the vistas from the road immeasurable. The houses in the valleys below the road stood well apart from one another and changed in structure from cinder blocks to mud bricks. In several of the villages the homes were decorated with triangles or circles applied in ochre, and small round storage sheds stood nearby, each capped by a tall, straw dome. Every quarter of a mile or so, often far from any discernable village, they passed someone walking down the road carrying on their head a load of water or charcoal or sticks for fire. And at the curves, they often passed vendors selling burlap bags of charcoal, watermelon or ears of roasted corn.

It began to rain, but they pressed on. The ruts in the road started filling with water, and then the entire road became a water-filled swale. Jabari put the Land Cruiser in four-wheel drive and plowed through. They traveled at agonizingly slow speeds for fifteen kilometers.

"Does it always rain like this?" Aaron asked.

"No sir, the rainy season is just beginning," Jabari said. "It is most strange to see so much rain so soon."

"How long does the rainy season last?" Anna asked.

"It will rain some afternoons this month; next month heavy skies and much rain, then less and less. Then we don't see rain until the small rains in October."

"Jabari! Watch out!" Aaron shouted. A tanker truck with some hundred sheaves of maize tied in bundles across the top swerved in their direction. Jabari turned quickly to the left, landed in a ditch and stopped just short of a huddle of people, their heads bowed against the slanting rain.

The people shouted, waved fists at the car then moved aside. Jabari drove slowly, half in the ditch, until he found a low spot in the crumbling pavement and eased the Land Cruiser back onto the road. They crawled through the dwindling light. Jabari said they wouldn't make it all the way to Ahadi at this pace, and there were no towns with hotels nearby.

Anna wanted to rewind the day; turn back to Dar Es Salaam, erase their long trip from Boston, their arrival in Dar, their meeting with the Sikes, their trip through the city slums. She wanted to go back three weeks in time and tell Aaron no, she wouldn't come. It was a harebrained idea to go to Africa. Reckless. Even dangerous. What could they accomplish here that they couldn't accomplish more effectively at home?

Jabari spoke up, interrupting her thoughts. "I know a place we can stay if the road is not too bad. There's a mission that's like a small hotel. They will find us a bed for the night."

"What kind of mission?" Aaron asked.

"They are people from America," he said. "Some kind of Jesus people."

Aaron grinned. "Aren't you afraid they'll try to convert you?"

Jabari rubbed his finger across his mustache and grinned in return. "We won't be there long enough," he said.

"How far?" Aaron asked.

"Maybe forty-five minutes, after stopping for gas."

Aaron tilted his head to get Anna's opinion. She nodded. "Let's go," he said.

Anna nodded because she was tired and becoming afraid. The road was hazardous; it was getting dark. Since they couldn't turn back now, she would welcome what refuge they might find. Yet she wondered about these Jesus people who left the comforts at home to provide a haven for poor or stranded travelers—a room at the inn. Did they unconditionally welcome people of any or no faith—or would they try to urge them into their particular fold? Was the God she knew best, the Episcopal God, watching over her and Aaron on this treacherous night, and, if so, was He equally protective of Jabari, a Muslim?

She respected American congregations for their commitment to destitute people living in distant lands and admired their work in education, medicine, well digging, home building. She'd seen many forms of religion in her travels, had observed societies devoted to vastly different gods, yet struggled to understand why each religion seemed to offer salvation only to adherents of their own faith. She wondered how many wars had been fought, how many lives needlessly sacrificed due to religious intolerance.

She closed her eyes. Which god was the true god? Any of the ancient gods of Olympus? One of the seven lucky gods of Japan? The often-vengeful God of the Old Testament? Yahweh? Brahma? Christianity's Holy Trinity? Allah? The Rastafarian Jah? The Sikhs' Ram? The Jesus who appeared to Joseph Smith? The ancestors who safeguard an African village? She wondered if none of them were true, or if all were true by virtue of existing in the minds of believers.

§§§

When she opened her eyes, they were pulling into an Agip

station to refuel. While Jabari pumped gas, she went to the bathroom, but the stench from the hole-in-the ground toilet left her gagging. She ran to the food concession counter where Aaron was hunched under the awning, sheltered from the rain. The smell of samosas frying in rank grease churned her stomach even more. When Aaron asked her what she wanted to eat, she swallowed hard, shook her head, swallowed again and told him she was going to the car. "But I could use something to drink," she said, and studied the row of bottles lined up over the grill. "A Fanta Orange," she said. "Now."

Aaron looked at her closely, handed her his bottle of Sprite. "Try this instead. I think it will work better."

Anna took the soda and made it to the car as Jabari was replacing the nozzle on the gas pump. She curled up in the back seat while he paid the attendant and joined Aaron at the food counter. After opening the window a crack for fresh air and taking a few swallows of the soda, she'd convinced her stomach to settle.

Half an hour beyond the gas station Jabari turned off the main road onto a lane that had become a river of red mud and was littered with stones and logs which he circumvented with extreme care.

The sky was black, the rain relentless, and the wipers smeared mud across the windshield. Jabari peered intently down the road. Finally, a single light bulb appeared on a pole ahead on the left, and beneath it a faded red hand-painted sign:

Njoo kwa Ujumbe wa Yesu
Kitanda na Kifungua Kinywa
Come to Jesus Mission
Bed & Breakfast

The path narrowed into one lane of slick mud, and they crept for another ten minutes until ahead was a squat L-shaped building made of gray cement block with a dozen small wooden doors strung down each wing. At the front of the first building was a larger door and, to the side of the door, a picture window—the only window Anna could see. The room was lit, and inside were tables and chairs and a small reception desk. Though it was past nine o'clock, Anna could see the heads of several people.

"Not exactly the Savoy," Aaron said. "But at least it seems to be open, and there appear to be quite a few rooms— and only a couple of cars."

They parked as close to the lobby door as possible and stepped out into rain and mud which flowed through the laces of Anna's sneakers.

Above the door was another roughly-painted sign, this one in blue outlined in gold:

Kukubaliana Kama Kristo Amekukubali
Waroma 15:7
Therefore Welcome One Another
as Christ Has Welcomed You
Romans 15:7

Aaron began to untie his shoes, but a bright Southern female voice called out: "Welcome to Jesus! And y'all leave on your shoes. No foot washin' being offered tonight."

Anna peered around the door. Standing beside a folding chair at one of the oblong tables was a middle-aged woman with thin threads of gray-streaked brown hair drooping from her long, narrow head. For so long a face, her nose seemed remarkably small. Her cerulean eyes were intense, piercing.

The woman laughed aloud, and the small black boy sitting next to her giggled. As he opened his mouth, his top teeth protruded half an inch beyond the lower. A thin man sitting across from them wore baggy jeans held up by wide red suspenders looped over his slumped shoulders. He looked at Anna's muddy feet and scowled. "Just maybe we oughtta commence a foot washing right now," he said.

The woman came to the door. "I'm Tallulah Patton from Eureka Springs, Arkansas. Ever heard of Eureka Springs?"

When Anna's parents were having it out with each other her junior year of high school in Tidewater, Virginia, they sent her to St. Mary's Academy in Little Rock, where her Aunt Constance lived and could keep an eye out for her. Her roommate's grandparents—the Skeltons—had a vacation home in Eureka Springs, and she was sometimes invited as a house guest.

"I've actually been there," Anna said. "Did you ever hear of Judge Joe Skelton?"

Tallulah's eyes lit up. "I sure did hear tell of him. Had a fancy place on Beaver Lake. Fancy Grand Banks trawler, biggest thing on the lake, as I recall. But the Skeltons wasn't stuck up like so many of them summer folk. In fact, he left a goodly sum to the mission effort, God rest his soul."

Anna was surprised that Judge Skelton would leave the mission a bequest. He took her and her roommate fishing on Sunday mornings and usually had a tee time at the Prairie Creek Golf Club Sunday afternoons. He never indicated he was sorry to be missing a sermon.

"We only had one other guest here ever even heard of Eureka Springs," Tallulah said. "That paper mill lady with the red hair. Had kinfolk that worked for Walmart over in Bentonville." She turned to the thin man who was still scowling at Anna's mucky feet. "What's her name, Salem?"

He rubbed a slender finger around in his ear. "Can't rightly recall."

"We are hoping there might be a couple of rooms available," Aaron said. "The road was pretty much washed out, and we knew we wouldn't make it to Ahadi tonight. We're really tired."

"Well, bless your hearts. Y'all must be paper mill folks, too!"

Tallulah joined them at the reception desk at the front of the room and peered at a drawing of the property. Aaron placed his left hand on top of the desk. Anna assumed he was displaying his wedding ring on purpose. "We are Mr. and Mrs. Chadwick," Aaron said, "and would like a double room if you have it. Our friend, Mr. Tamin, needs a single room."

"The Lord will provide," she said.

"And how much will the Lord require to provide?" he asked.

Tallulah smiled up at Aaron. "Your faith in Him and 5,000 shillings for the double room. All the rooms are the same size, but for only one person it's 3,500 shillings."

Aaron took out his wallet and counted out 9,000 shillings in 1,000-shilling notes. Anna calculated quickly, figuring the cost to be about $20 U.S. dollars. It's definitely not the Savoy, she thought, but she was tired and grateful for a bed.

Tallulah handed Aaron a registration form and placed his change on the counter. On the greasy blue 500-shilling note was a picture of an angry water buffalo. Aaron gave her back the note. "A small donation," he said.

She clasped the note in her hands. "Why, bless you, Mr. Chadwick."

She picked up a pen and marked a room near the lobby with XX. She examined the drawing again, then marked an X on a room in the middle of the other wing. Finally, she reached into a drawer, turned a lock and extracted two keys.

"The Lord be praised, a simple breakfast will be served here in the worship hall between 8:00 and 9:00 in the morning," she said and led them to the door. The rain was gushing from the eaves, and they hesitated before running to the car.

Anna wondered if Tallulah would send them off with an evening prayer, and in her head repeated the words she was required to say every night as a child: *If I should die before I wake, I pray the Lord my soul to take.*

As if for the first time, Anna realized how terrifying it must have been to close her eyes and repeat these words. She wondered why she was made to learn this prayer, to believe she might not wake up to see the next day. What nightmares resulted? What fears? In a flash, she saw another religious enclave and all those children lying dead in Jonestown, Guyana. But this was not the People's Temple. And Tallulah was no Jim Jones.

Whether or not it was the Lord who had kept her, she'd awakened every morning since, and she had no option but to trust that she would wake up tomorrow and the next day and all the days she and Aaron remained in this rough land. She was certain that they would survive, despite the unknown dangers that lay ahead.

Tallulah wished them a blessed night, handed over two keys, pointed out the way to the rooms and went back inside.

§§§

The room was sparse and recently painted white with a slight tinge of green. There were no windows. A lime-green curtain served as the door to the bathroom. Anna opened the curtain; behind it was a white plastic stall shower, a small sink and a low, sit-down toilet.

Against the opposite wall were two single beds. The table between them was just big enough for a small lamp and a Swahili Bible. Above the table was a picture of Jesus, the sun setting on a purple mountain behind him. Jesus was presiding over a table loaded with loaves of bread and stacks of bright, silver fish, but he was not looking at the table. He appeared to be looking at everything in the room at once.

Anna put her suitcase on the end of the first bed and peered closely at the picture. "He's judging us," she said.

Aaron put down his bag, looked briefly at the painting and shook his head. "He's blessing us," he said. He paused. "At least I hope he's blessing us."

Aaron took a shower and was in bed when Anna emerged from the bathroom. He was lying flat on his back, his shoulders filling the whole width of the bed, and his feet hanging over the baseboard. Clearly, there was not room for her to snuggle up next to him.

Maybe she couldn't thrive here on love alone, but she believed her rekindled love for Aaron would play a major role in her life story, no matter how the plot unfolded. So, she nudged him and told him to turn on his side. She removed her robe, turned out the light on the table and climbed in beside him.

In that space, no wider, no softer than a church pew, under the indifferent gaze of all those fish, under Jesus's watchful gaze, Aaron embraced her, held her, kissed her there and there—and there—and they made love, no gap between them, the two of them no longer disparate individuals, but joined that night in an unaccustomed but assuring way.

A Tanzanian Story

CHAPTER FIVE: A NEW NAME

$\mathcal{T}$he rain had ended during the night, and the morning sun was glimmering through high, thin clouds. After Tallulah's breakfast of watered-down gruel, they slowly made their way back to the main road.

They turned at the eucalyptus forest and climbed past the tea plantation. The temperature dropped degree by degree. They finally reached the top of a steep ridge rising 2,000 feet above the valley. Beyond were grasslands, gently rolling hills and distant mountains. The sky was boundless and clear, and they stopped for a few moments to look across some 160 kilometers where the Kipengere Range, part of the East African Rift, rose from the northern end of Lake Nyasa.

Anna imagined standing on the edge of this precipice with a telephoto lens, searching the vast and inscrutable landscape, exploring the rocks and crevasses for a connection—human, animal, even a single bright flower. But as hard as she tried to imagine what lay hidden before her, all she could see were barren hillsides and silent grasslands.

They returned to the car and traveled a little farther—down a steep incline, up again, around a series of S-curves—then stopped once more. Below them in the valley was an expanse of scrubland where, alongside the tracks of the Tazara Railway, sprawled the multi-colored concrete and steel buildings, the rust-stained towers, silos, cat walks and conveyer belts of a pulp and paper complex, one of

East Africa's largest, most prestigious, and most costly development projects. No smoke rose from the towers.

Aaron stared down at the mill, took a deep breath, exhaled. He smoothed back the lock of hair that had fallen across his forehead and placed his hand on Anna's shoulder. "Oh, Anna, what have I done to us?" he said. He shook his head but said no more.

They circled the valley, bare but for a few mud homes, then descended and drove slowly past the mill site. Just beyond were a half-dozen squat cement-block buildings surrounding a dirt courtyard. "That's the primary school," Jabari said.

Next he pointed out a field of crops bordered by a wire fence. "That's our *shamba*. Everyone who works at the mill can grow a little food there."

Jabari drove the car slowly up the hillside where row upon close row of earthen-colored houses, topped with tin roofs, accommodated some 1,500 people—mill workers and their extended families. They passed a gray-haired woman carrying a large basket on her head; a group of barefoot children tumbling down a slope, their voices electric with pleasure. Anna peered at them closely. Even at play, rolling down a grassy hill, their clothes looked clean, and they looked healthy.

Ahead of them a young man wobbled up the hill on a rusty bicycle. A tall woman on a blue scooter edged past him and waved as the Land Cruiser went by. Jabari waved back. Anna was intrigued by the woman on the scooter, feeling she must be someone of stature; someone with a sense of independence, and she asked Jabari if he knew who the woman was. "Yes," he said. "That is Grace Kapera riding her *pikipiki*. She is the very fine head mistress of the primary school we just passed."

The houses increased in size, street by street. Near the top of the hill, beyond a closed dispensary and empty tennis court, curved Etruscan tiles formed the roofs, and gardens flourished behind mud walls. Jabari told them that the few remaining expatriates and senior indigenous workers lived in these fine homes.

At the top of the hill he parked outside the largest house of all, the front door banked by an explosion of red and orange canna lilies, white calla lilies, succulents, impatiens, birds of paradise—an opulent display against stained white plaster. Anna's first impression of Glenna Sikes' garden turned out to be more—much more—than she expected. It was almost like a work of art, nearly finished, already enchanting.

As she bent to inspect the flower of a particularly robust bird of paradise, a small, white-faced cat peered around the corner of the house, meowed and gave them a knowing look before retreating through the thick bougainvillea hedge.

Aaron retrieved a key from his pocket and unlocked the front door. He turned on the dim yellow overhead light, and Jabari rolled their two suitcases across large, white stone tiles. The house smelled stuffy, like a trunk in an attic, opened for the first time in years. The middle of the room was bare, though a Craftsman-style desk, loveseat and two matching chairs were lined up against the far wall. The furniture was stenciled in bold white letters with TPM, the company initials, followed by GM and a series of numbers. The chairs had been stripped of pillows; the loveseat had no slipcover.

Curtain hooks dangled across the top of the louvered windows, but there were no curtains, not in the living room, dining room, kitchen; not in any of the four bedrooms down the hall. In the first bedroom there was only an empty yellow refrigerator plugged into the wall. In the second, a plain wood desk was shoved up against the window. In each of the two back bedrooms a double bed faced a single dresser. There were no sheets or bedspreads. No rugs. No shower curtains or towels in either bathroom. Fissured nail holes remained where pictures had hung and, most surprising of all, twelve holes studded the kitchen windowsill, the cup hooks removed.

Anna opened the kitchen cabinets to find a dented saucepan, a warped frying pan and a large encrusted stock pot, no lid. She checked the drawers: two knives, two forks, no spoons. Seven spatulas.

She didn't expect to find a dishwasher, yet there it was, along with a clean oven. Beyond the kitchen breezeway were the servants' quarters—a bathroom with a small shower stall and two small square bedrooms, one empty except for an army cot and one filled with four chest freezers, three apparently working. There was no sign of Tobias, the houseman and cook.

Aaron collapsed into the loveseat and rubbed his thumb across his forehead. He closed his eyes. "Jabari," he said. "When you picked up the Sikes, did the house look like this? I was told it was fully furnished."

Jabari explained that the Sikes used the curtains, slip covers, rugs and linens to wrap goods for their container shipment home. "They brought so many things with them from America," he said. His eyes grew narrower with each item he listed: "Blue dishes and silver pots; carpets and tins and tins of food and ....

"And what of Tobias?" Aaron asked.

Jabari looked down at the stone floor. "On the way to Dar Es Salaam he told me Mama Sikes was going to find

44

him a job at a hotel in town."

Aaron opened his eyes and nodded. "Thank you, Jabari. I'll drive you home. I want to run down to the mill."

Jabari zipped up his jacket and held out the car keys. "I live just four streets down," he said. "I can walk home, sir."

"No, you've had a long couple of days, and you have a heavy bag to carry. I'll take you." Aaron slowly unfolded his lean six feet, two inches from the loveseat. Jabari turned to Anna and smiled, his eyes bright, sincere. "*Karibu* to Ahadi, Mama GM."

Anna felt she had just been officially welcomed to the village. She had a new name, a title: Mama GM. It was almost as if she had been re-christened. She replied with two of the dozen Swahili words she had memorized. "*Asante sana.*"

Since she didn't yet feel comfortable with the Swahili words leaving her tongue, she added the English translation. "Thank you very much."

"*Wewe ni kuwakaribisha sana*, Mama," he replied.

§§§

When the sound of the Land Cruiser disappeared into the distance, the house became chillingly quiet. As Anna rolled her suitcase down the hallway, she was startled by a foot-long green gecko lizard slithering across the wall. He darted his red tongue at her, slipped down to the floor and fled around the corner into the first bedroom where he hid behind the yellow refrigerator.

Anna continued down the hall, her sandals tapping too loudly on the hard floors. She entered the largest bedroom at the back of the house and opened the closet door, but there were no hangers. She took the clothes from her suitcase and stuffed them into the two bottom dresser drawers, leaving the top drawers for Aaron. She put her suitcase in the closet and wandered through the house. With each step she became more dismayed.

She returned to the back bedroom and peered through the window. The light was fading, and men's voices rose in the distance—voices, then laughter, silence, then more laughter closer by. At that wary moment she was grateful for the black iron bars set horizontally every four inches into the casements as protection from intruders. But what she saw beyond the bars was astonishing, and, when Aaron returned an hour later, his shoulders hunched, his eyes worried, she beckoned him out the patio door.

Twilight was settling on the roses, the hydrangeas and hibiscus. The setting sun shimmered across thirty-foot high morning glories, through the banana trees, over the pineapples and sweet potato vines; dappled the peppers. The cool air was fragrant with mingling scents: sweet and flowery and pungent. The only light except for a shy three-quarter moon was a single fire beside a house on the distant hillside.

A deep-throated bird called from the edge of the garden. From the valley, a like bird answered.

As Aaron and Anna nestled together on the porch swing, the first star appeared, and while they continued to hold fast to each other, the sky became saturated with stars—more stars than Anna had ever seen in a night sky. In fact, the stars within the Milky Way seemed so dense there appeared to be little room between them to accommodate more. Four stars glowed brighter than all the others: the Southern Cross. How inconsequential Anna felt; how trifling the temporary lack of curtains and cup hooks.

Finally, they went inside and, using the last match in a box on the mantle, Aaron lit the two logs remaining in the fireplace. In their bedroom, he hung shirts from the bare curtain hooks, and they eased down onto the hard, naked mattress. Through gaps in the clothes hung from the top of the window, Anna gazed at the stars—stars so far away and yet so bright it seemed as if she could beckon them, bring them close, touch them, even hold them in her hand.

A Tanzanian Story

CHAPTER SIX: THE BUSH SNAKE

*E*arly the next morning, while Aaron was shaving, Anna strolled through the vegetable garden which sprawled across a third of an acre behind the servants' quarters to the right of the house. Wide paths delineated rows of peanuts, fruit and vegetables, and a row of lemon, mango and banana trees, a coconut palm grew along the far walkway. Despite Glenna Sikes' concern, the garden appeared to be intact, nothing uprooted, nothing stolen. Anna picked two ripe bananas, an almost-ripe tomato and a green pepper.

Back inside, she found three eggs in the refrigerator, and, when she cracked them open, they smelled okay. So did the small bottle of congealed cooking oil. There was a coffee pot, but she couldn't find any coffee. She filled the dented saucepan with water from the filter cannister sitting on the counter and set the pot on the stove to boil. When it began to bubble, she moved the pot to a cold burner and added two tea bags. She was relieved to discover two chipped mugs and a stack of paper plates in the back of a cupboard.

Anna was dishing the omelet and banana slices onto the plates when Aaron came into the kitchen. He was dressed in a blue sport jacket and knotting the red tie he usually wore when negotiating with financiers.

"Expecting bankers?" She asked

He smiled. "No, but I figured I might need some extra muscle today."

His light brown hair was dark, damp, and smelled like Prell shampoo.

"You took a shower? How did you dry off?"

He tapped his temple with his index finger and gave Anna a crafty grin. "An old bushman's trick," he said. "Jockey shorts. Two. I left two dry pairs for you."

He noticed the plates of food. "What miracle have you wrought here, woman?" He leaned down to kiss her, and she held the kiss as long as she could.

While they ate, Aaron said he would figure out how to procure the sheets and towels and dishes which should have been part of the furnishings. He'd ask the mill manager, Lance Fuller, for some food staples until they could get to Iringa on the weekend. He took a sip of the tea then shook his head. "And some coffee," he added. "Lots of coffee."

Aaron stood up, stretched his arms around Anna in a close hug, picked up his overstuffed briefcase and headed for the door. He opened the lock and straightened his shoulders before peering back at her. His amber eyes were both thoughtful and determined; his expression optimistic. "I'll see you at noon or shortly thereafter," he said. "I love you, Mama GM."

Anna called back to him to tell him she loved him, too, but he was already out the door.

She headed down the hall and looked into the bathroom. There was a long pair of jeans covering the window and two pairs of damp jockey shorts hanging from the shower curtain rod. Two pairs of dry shorts lay folded at the edge of the single free-standing sink. She needed a shower but decided to leave the shorts for Aaron and pulled a Vermont College tee-shirt from her drawer. She used the shirt, along with a small bar of airline soap from Aaron's shaving kit, to wash off the grime.

As she put the breakfast dishes in the sink to dry, she

heard a rustling outside and went to the back door. The yard extended to a perimeter hedge, high enough to shield the house from passersby on the adjacent road, low enough to reveal the valley, escarpment and mountains beyond. Glenna Sikes had obviously spared nothing to make her garden impressive. Morning glories, lilies and daisies of all colors grew in a long row in front of the hedge. Roses and hibiscus bordered the patio, and exotic purple and yellow orchids climbed the posts.

A lanky young man was swinging a sharp-bladed panga across the lawn. With each rhythmic swing, his muscles swelled, and blades of cut grass flew into the air. There was so much grass between the patio and the far hedge that Anna wondered how many hours it took to cut, and why there was no lawn mower to make the job easier.

As soon as she stepped off the patio, the gardener bowed, ran toward her and leaned forward on the panga. He appeared to be in his mid-twenties, with a wide smile, long, straight nose and animated eyes. His skin was bright, like polished cherry wood. "*Jambo*, Mama GM," he said. "I am Hami Kamala."

"*Jambo*," she replied. She had assumed there would be help in this large garden, and Hami appeared to be very capable help.

"Mama, my English—" He lowered his head and paused a moment, searching for the words. "Not good," he finally said.

Hami struggled to find the words to tell Anna he'd been the GM's gardener for a year and lived two streets down the hill with his uncle, Mahib Kamala, who designed and maintained the township plantings, and had helped create this garden as well.

Anna realized that Hami's English was not as bad as he claimed. In fact, it improved markedly as he anxiously asked: "Mama, will there be some small bites at lunch for Tobias and me?"

"Tobias? But he is gone. Doesn't he have a new job in the city?"

Hami continued in a faltering pidgin, telling Anna that Tobias went to Dar Es Salaam with the Sikes but left his wife and child at home some five kilometers toward the valley and had no intention of moving to the city where he couldn't plant and harvest his own *shamba*, receive company pay and monthly bonuses from the GM.

"Then why did he go to Dar?" Anna asked. Hami looked down at the ground, as if formulating his words carefully, then nodded. "He went because Mama Sikes said he must go there to find a good job. Tobias, he was afraid for making her angry."

Anna wondered if Glenna Sikes was worried about Tobias' future. Or did Glenna want to remove him, like the curtains and cup hooks, from this house? But Anna tried to dismiss the idea, knowing she was being unfair. Still, it bothered her that Tobias didn't tell Glenna the truth.

Anna assured Hami that when they had food, he and Tobias, if he showed up, would certainly have food.

Hami returned to cutting the grass. His pace seemed to have increased twofold. But then he suddenly jumped back, stopped and peered straight down. He stabbed the sharp end of the panga into the ground and rolled it back and forth. When he lifted it, a ten-foot snake wriggled from the blade. He balanced the snake on the panga, took it to the edge of the garden and slung it across the hedge.

Anna had read about Africa's deadly black mambas,

green mambas; about pythons and cobras and boomslangs.

"Hami!" she shouted. "What snake was that?"

"I think only a bush snake, Mama." Anna wondered if it was, indeed, just a bush snake. She hoped Hami was telling her the truth.

§§§

Just before eleven o'clock, Anna heard a car pulling into the driveway and unlocked the front door to see a red Suzuki jeep parked outside. The driver, a short, slightly-stooped Tanzanian wearing a tan safari suit, darted from the right-hand driver's seat to left-side passenger door and opened it. A robust woman who appeared to be in her late fifties emerged from the car and headed toward the door. She had skin as pale as egg whites, large brown eyes, short, bright-red hair and was nonchalantly waving a stiff fan across her face. The fan, like those handed out on sweltering Sundays in the American South, pictured Jesus rising through a rift in billowing clouds. Her nails were manicured and painted orange-red, matching her lipstick and nearly identical to her hair color. She was wearing a white cotton skirt with a peasant blouse, and her white string purse jounced across her hip as she listed a little right then left stepping over the threshold.

"Hello, hello," the woman said. "I'm Priscilla Fuller. Welcome to the end of the earth!" Her voice was high, loud. The words were stretched, the tone cocky, the accent clearly Southern.

It took Anna a few seconds to recognize her name, then she realized her visitor was the wife of the mill manager, Lance Fuller.

"Priscilla, come in. I'm Anna Chadwick."

"I know, sweetie! I know! We've been expecting you for

a week! Where in the world have y'all been, Annie?"

"It's Anna."

Priscilla shrugged, looked around the barren room, rolled her eyes and let loose a brassy laugh.

"Glenna didn't leave y'all much, did she? Oh, you poor dear. But you'll be just dandy when your container shipment arrives." She frowned. "Of course, ours took two and a half months."

For all employees stationed in rural areas overseas, the company allowed them an air shipment as well as a 20-foot container shipped by sea. Anna and Aaron knew they couldn't transport their Vermont home to Tanzania, nor did they want to, so they opted out of the sea container.

"Um. Priscilla, well, you see, we didn't actually pack a container," Anna said.

Priscilla looked at Anna as if she were an extraterrestrial.

"The air shipment seemed enough to handle what we need."

"To each his own," Priscilla said. "Just wait until you're dying for some good ole Ritz crackers." She started rummaging through her purse but was interrupted as her driver called through the screen door: "*Hodi! Hodi!*"

"Bring the basket on inside," Priscilla said. The driver was carrying a large round basket tied at the top with strands of sisal. "Now take it on into the kitchen, Daniel."

Daniel looked at Anna quickly, as if asking permission to enter.

"*Karibu*," Anna said. Daniel nodded, then hesitated and looked at Anna as if really seeing her for the first time. "*Karibu* to Ahadi, Mama GM," he said. Anna was welcomed again, named again, and, again, she was grateful.

"*Asante sana*, Daniel." This time she felt no need to

translate.

Daniel turned toward the hallway. Priscilla pointed to the right. "No, that way, Daniel." He turned around and scurried toward the kitchen, his shoulders slumping a bit more. He put the basket on the counter and stood there, staring at the dishwasher.

"None of them have half a brain," Priscilla muttered, then bellowed into the kitchen: "You can wait out in the car, Daniel. I'll be done in just a minute."

Anna stepped back and turned her head to distance herself from Priscilla.

After Daniel retreated out the front door, Priscilla plucked a sheet of thin newsprint from her purse and thrust it in Anna's face. "Six thousand, fifty-five Tanzanian shillings," she said. "I paid her, so, I'm sorry, dear, but money being tight as it is, you're gonna have to pay me back."

She handed over a receipt signed in blue ink. The distinctively British signature read Catherine Dennison. "What's this for?" Anna asked.

"The basket."

"The basket Daniel just took into the kitchen?"

Priscilla nodded. "Mama Dennison. From her farm. We buy a basket every week—a hunk of meat and 5 kilos of vegetables. Sometimes the meat is edible. Usually rump. Sometimes lamb. Sometimes tongue. Uggh." She stuck out her tongue. "But at least it's fairly clean—not like what you get in the market. I picked up the baskets yesterday. Should still be fresh enough."

"Who is Mama Dennison?"

"An old British bird. Has a big farm over toward Iringa. We take turns going down to get our baskets. Your turn is next week."

"Look, I'm sorry. We've only just arrived, and I haven't changed any money."

Priscilla's eyes lit up. "I'll give you a break if you have a twenty dollar US bill," she said.

"I don't have a twenty and have no idea of the conversion rate, but you'll be repaid one way or the other tomorrow."

"Whatever," Priscilla said, scowling. She turned toward the door.

As much as Anna wanted the woman to vanish, she knew she had an obligation to be hospitable to Aaron's employees and their families, so she made a half-hearted gesture to invite her to stay. "I'd like to offer you something, but all I have … some tea?"

Priscilla turned, sniffed the room, waved her fan and shook her head. "This place smells as if it's been locked up for a whole dang year! Gotta go. Bridge at the tea plantation this afternoon." She hesitated, then looked at Anna hopefully. "You play bridge?"

Anna shook her head. "I'm sorry. No."

"Too bad. Bridge sure helps pass the time. Dinner at the Barnetts tonight. B-20. Next row directly down. Six-thirty. Nice to meet ya, dear." She turned abruptly and marched out of the house. Daniel raced to open the car door.

Anna called out after her. "Oh, Priscilla. Please. Wait."

Priscilla turned and frowned, clearly annoyed at being stopped.

"I'm sorry to hold you up, but Aaron was going to talk to your husband about borrowing a bit of food. I guess we're set with the basket, and there seems to be a good deal ripening in the garden, but could you loan us some coffee until we can get to Iringa?"

"Okay. Yep. I'll have Daniel bring it right to you when he

returns your car after I get back from bridge."

"My car?"

"The Suzuki here."

Priscilla settled into the passenger seat and rolled down the window. "You're the only one with two cars assigned," she said. "Since y'all weren't here...well, rank and privilege."

She rolled up the window. Daniel started the Suzuki with a jerk. It jounced down the incline. Anna wondered how Priscilla managed to appropriate her car, if it truly was her car, and if so, where she would go in it.

She paced the road in front of the house. She was here only because Aaron was here. Would she ever feel as if she belonged? Would she fit in? Did she even want to try?

What about her new African neighbors? Would she ever understand the thoughts they pondered as they walked from the village to the market and back? Would she be better off taking up bridge?

She stopped and studied the flowers—a colorful parade of red and yellow lilies beside an assertive cluster of birds of paradise. She reminded herself to be patient and open to all possibilities. If nothing else, she had a garden to tend.

She went inside and was heading toward the kitchen to open the basket, but, instead, turned toward the back patio. Hami was still swinging his panga across the grass, and the white-faced cat was lounging on the rocking chair, twitching her small pink ears. There was a notch in her right ear, a swathe of black fur forming a butterfly across the top of her head, and her tail was thoroughly black as well. She looked up at Anna and squealed, as if vexed at Anna's intrusion.

When Anna approached her, the cat jumped from the chair and hid behind a post. Anna called to Hami. "Who

57

owns this cat?"

Hami ran to Anna and stooped down to peer at the cat. "I never see this *paca* until this same moment," he said.

The cat wailed, then jumped back up on the chair, showing off her little lion teeth.

"Okay, Simba," Anna said to the cat. "If you stick around, I'll find you some small bites of food and hopefully some milk as well. Maybe we'll figure out a way to become friends. Maybe we'll have some interesting conversations."

CHAPTER SEVEN: ORNGES

*J*ust inside the entrance to the Barnett's house stood a tall ebony carving of a dozen men and women, intertwined and climbing over a wave of bark. Becky Barnett greeted Anna and Aaron at the door and said the carving was characteristic work of the Makonde tribe, living in Southeast Tanzania and Mozambique, and the figures represented slaves trying to escape. Anna looked closer and realized that some of the figures had their hands bound behind their backs. Their faces conveyed anguish and fear.

Steve Barnett appeared, introduced himself to Anna and waylaid Aaron. Anna followed Becky into the living room where she was drawn to an array of roughly-carved masks hung over the fireplace. She was especially taken with the smallest mask. The mouth—a perfect oh!—comprised half the face, and the eyes, though mere slits, seemed to see beyond where eyes can see.

Becky was shorter than Anna by several inches, and her light brown hair was stippled with gray. Her hazel eyes flickered intelligently from object to object, person to person, never settling for long, as if quickly appraising all she saw. Anna glanced back at Becky's husband, Steve, still talking to Aaron. He was tall with hair so blond it seemed almost white. His gray-blue eyes moved slowly, carefully.

Becky told Anna she'd graduated from Oberlin, and Steve had gone to St. Olaf. "We met on a plane headed for Uganda. Both of us had just joined the Peace Corps. After our training session, Steve was assigned to a fishing village on Lake Victoria. I was headed to an agricultural region in the North." Becky smiled, crinkles forming around her eyes.

"We said our goodbyes, and I stoically took a seat on the bus headed north. Within minutes, Steve was pushing his backpack under the seat next to me." She laughed. "He'd convinced the director to change his assignment. Steve said he told him he couldn't swim."

Anna hoped she had met a compatriot. But before she could tell Becky how much she loved this story, how she admired her for joining the Peace Corps, Becky was talking again.

"I'm studying Swahili. Sometimes I get a chance to help out at the primary school. The head mistress, Grace Kapera—you'll have to meet her—she has a little blue *piki-piki* she rides around the village." Becky laughed again.

"Yes, I saw her on her scooter on the road coming in," Anna said. "Can you introduce us?"

Becky turned her head toward the kitchen. "Gotta go check on dinner."

After Becky disappeared into the kitchen, Anna examined an exquisite piece of art sitting atop the standard-issue desk. It was a bust carved in multi-colored stone, perhaps serpentine. The figure was clearly a shaman with a cluster of intricately carved feathers emerging from his headband. His eyes were compassionate, and his appearance contemplative. Yet when Anna looked again, his expression had changed. From the left side, he appeared sorrowful, and from the right, hopeful. She stepped around him, from side to side—from sorrow to contemplation to hope.

After college, Anna's first job had been as a researcher at the Metropolitan Museum in New York. She would sometimes sneak away from her desk to gaze at Cezanne's *Gar-*

danne, the village wending uphill, much like Ahadi: patches of green, a purple tinge to the windows, the sky; the rise of barren land beyond the vacant town—the almost cubist feel—angles, squares, simplicity, tranquility, as if the homes, the trees, the church had risen from the earth without human interference.

She recalled a puzzling, unfinished feeling when she wandered out of the African collection of carvings, masks, bronzes—the rigid stances, incomprehensible expressions. She knew that many of the masks represented spirits, though they seemed to her to lack soul. She wished back then that she could see them as they were meant to be—human and animal faces worn by moving, dancing people who made the spirits come alive.

But looking at the bust of the shaman that night she felt she was seeing the human soul in all its complexity: contemplation, sorrow, hope.

She wondered if she could produce even one photograph to reveal the complexity found in this African soul.

§§§

In the dining room they seated themselves. Originally thirty expatriates held every supervisory job at the mill. Over the past four years they'd been replaced by Tanzanians. Now only Lance and Priscilla Fuller, Steve and Becky Barnett, Ryder McGowan, Aaron and Anna remained. Nine months hence, only she and Aaron would remain, provided the management contract was renewed.

Lance Fuller was a gentle, balding, soft-spoken foil to his brash wife, Priscilla. Ryder McGowan, the pulp mill manager, appeared to Anna to be in his early sixties. A gray safari jacket bulged across his paunch, and oversized horned rim glasses covered his pale blue eyes, shaggy eyebrows and flushed cheeks.

Lance turned toward Ryder who was sitting on his right. "What news from your wife, Bella?" he asked. Ryder just shrugged his shoulders.

"Pity she had to go back to the UK so soon," Priscilla said. Again, Ryder shrugged. They were halfway through the meal before Ryder McGowan finally spoke.

"Ornges," he said.

"What on earth are you talking about, Ryder?" Priscilla demanded.

"Ornges," he repeated.

"Are you talking about oranges?" Becky asked.

Ryder nodded. "Ornges. Mbeya."

Lance turned toward Ryder. "Are you saying there are oranges now in the market in Mbeya?"

Ryder nodded again. "Ornges."

Anna looked across at Aaron who eyed Ryder with concern then shook his head. She wondered how effective this man could be leading his team of Tanzanian workers. She visualized Ryder standing next to the chipper in the mill. "Wood," he said. Then she envisioned him next to the agitator. "Pulp," he said. She turned her head to hide her smile.

The meal seemed to Anna to be extravagant for the setting. There was ham from the smokehouse at the tea plantation, a smooth California Bordeaux, pineapple relish, fresh Brussels sprouts, scalloped potatoes and homemade strawberry cake.

After dinner, Becky handed Aaron a bag with leftover ham and potatoes, two eggs, a bottle of Cabernet, three-quarters of a quart of milk plus cutlery and dishes for two. She added a jar of Africafe, greatly appreciated since Priscilla neglected to send the coffee or the Suzuki back with Daniel.

Then Becky gave Anna a stapled sheaf of papers, a monograph her husband, Steve, had written. "I think you'll want to give this a read-through," she said.

§§§

It was dark when Anna and Aaron walked up the hill to their house. Like the night before, the only sounds were voices from a distance—and, again, only men's voices. Remembering the snake Hami tossed from the garden that morning, Anna watched the road in front of them for any sign of movement.

When they turned into their street, she described to Aaron the statue of the shaman—the changing expression as she moved around him: sorrow, contemplation, hope.

"Yes," he said. "Africa. So much sorrow. So much promise."

He stopped walking, turned around to face her, put down the bag of supplies from the Barnetts and wrapped his arms around her shoulders. He drew her so close she could feel his warmth, even feel his heart beating. She leaned into him, letting him bear her weight. "Promise," he said. "I just found out that's what this place is called."

"Promise?" she murmured into his chest.

"The village, Ahadi. It's a Swahili word for promise. And I promise... oh, Anna, do you have any idea how much I love you?"

As they embraced in the street, a porch light flashed on in a house below them. Aaron pulled away, picked up the bag, and they walked a little faster up the hill.

At home, Aaron made a cup of coffee, and Anna filled a bowl with milk, adding a few small chunks of ham. They went out to the patio, and she put the bowl down by the post where Simba had been lurking before they left for dinner.

Neither Aaron nor Anna had ever owned a cat. She wondered at their independence, their apparent lack of concern about their caregivers. She was certain that their dog, Murray, felt he was the most important member of the family.

Aaron glanced warily at the bowl of milk. "We're making friends with a cat?" he said. "Murray may never speak to us again."

"Don't tell him," Anna replied.

CHAPTER EIGHT: A SURPRISE

*A*nna woke up realizing that Aaron had left the bedroom. In a few minutes, he returned, kissed her gently, rubbed her hair and told her to go back to sleep. She wrapped her arms around his neck and pulled him toward her. He kissed her again then ducked out from her arms. "I love you," he said, stood up, straightened his blue and gold striped tie then glanced at her, smiling. "Later," he said and left, shutting the bedroom door.

She fell back upon the pillow, and when she woke up again, Simba was whining beneath the window, her mouth wide-open, showing nearly all her sharp teeth. Anna pulled on a pair of shorts and a tee shirt, picked up Simba's empty bowl from the patio and half filled it with milk before taking a shower, peeling a banana and making a cup of tea for herself.

On the desk pushed up against the wall was a phone. Anna lifted the receiver, but there was no dial tone. She checked the cord and tried again but couldn't get a connection. There was also a 16-inch television console next to the phone. Because she was curious, she plugged it in and turned the dials, but all that appeared was static noise and ever-descending black and white fuzz.

So here she was, this Thursday morning, without communication in a house at the top of a hill, a house with naked windows, exposed to anyone passing by. She thought of the many housewives in America, Africa, Russia, Italy, Japan, spending the morning exactly as she was—alone with a list of menial chores to be completed, a list of desires unfulfilled, and, above all, concern for a husband at work and a child away.

She missed her son, Christopher, greatly, his wide smile, youthful energy, unlimited supply of imagination and a life-time of plans to fulfill. He had Aaron's hair coloring and height, her blue eyes and slightly upturned nose. He had Aaron's inclination for adventure and her artistic bent. She wondered if Christopher and his girlfriend, Beryl, would be cross-country skiing this mid-March weekend; if they would take Murray with them. She could see Murray bounding along in their tracks.

She missed Christopher, yet she knew it was time to cut him loose. When she was his age, she'd headed directly from college in Pennsylvania to a job in New York City. She knew almost nobody there but found a roommate and an af-fordable apartment in the far West Village. In no time at all she knew her way around Manhattan and felt like a true New Yorker. Her childhood home in Tidewater, Virginia had long ceased to be home.

Anna stepped outside and looked down at rows of houses below her. The streets were empty. She wondered if Ahadi, this place called Promise, felt like home to anyone. Did the people who came here to work at the mill create a village together? Did the children grow up feeling this is where their children and grandchildren belonged? More likely, she surmised, their roots would be firmly planted with their tribe in the village where their mother or father was born; where generation after generation of their ancestors emerged from the woods, hovered over the fields, protected the homes and the people inside.

Anna's villages spanned North America, but she felt

she no longer belonged to any of them. There was no place where generations of people would celebrate her return.

She'd lived in Virginia, Pennsylvania, New York, briefly in Arkansas, Connecticut, Vermont. Her father was born in San Francisco; her mother grew up in the Ozark hills. Her grandparents moved to the gulf coast of Florida where they died and were buried. Going back, far enough, her ancestral home was Devon, England and Stuttgart, Germany; and even further back perhaps a Tuscan valley, an island off Greece, a Russian steppe—even further back to a place somewhere in Africa, a village by a river or on a wind-swept plain, where the first cell of who she would become appeared in a long-ago mother.

§§§

Anna made the bed with the sheets which, along with a stack of rough white towels, mysteriously appeared on their door-step early that morning. Then she picked up Simba's bowl and filled it again with milk, added two chunks of ham and laid it down by the post. Simba bared her teeth, sprung at the bowl and gulped the milk. Then she turned her head, whim-pered and dove in again. Finally, she looked up at Anna and timidly, softly, briefly purred.

Hami was hunched over the flower garden along the far hedge, and, beyond him a layer of heavy clouds hovered across the valley below. She felt a gentle breeze, followed by a chilling mist, and went inside for a rain jacket and her cam-era. She was surprised to feel unexpected confidence as her right palm wrapped around the grip of the Cannon EOS-1.

Because she wanted to capture the subtle variations of tone and texture in the valley, the black and white film load-ed in the camera would work just fine. She walked to the back of the garden and played with the zoom and aperture settings. By lowering the f-stop to 1.4 and zooming out, she got a decent shot of a calla lily, the flower sharp and all the rest in soft focus. Then she opened the aperture to capture the full drama of clouds drifting across the valley. She knelt and took a picture of Hami silhouetted against the broad sky. He was the focal point, just right of the center of the image, and loomed over his surroundings. She thought she would be pleased when she had a chance to develop this final shot.

§§§

Anna went inside to check the beef from Mrs. Dennison. It had been tenderizing in slices of mango for nearly a day. She rummaged through Aaron's suitcase, found his bowie knife and carved the beef into cubes. She added potatoes, carrots and beans from the basket, diced tomatoes from the garden, and a cup of red wine from the bottle Becky had given them. She put the stew in the stock pot, turned the burner on low, made a second cup of tea then settled into the rocker on the patio to read the monograph Steve Barnett had written.

"Some two million years ago, the first human may have been born in what is now Tanzania. Yet it wasn't until the year 100 that the Bantu-speaking people then populating the region encountered their first outsiders. Arabs were establishing overland trade routes linking the coasts of East and West Africa and bringing with them a new culture and religion along with beads and cloth to exchange for ivory and gold—a poor exchange for the Bantus.

"In 1498, Vasco da Gama explored East Africa, and the Portuguese who followed established a base on the island of Zanzibar just off the coast. Some two hundred years later they were ousted by Arabs. In 1884 the German Colonisation Society began acquiring territory on the mainland. During World War I, British, Belgian and South African troops

occupied most of German East Africa, and, in 1916, the League of Nations turned the country—then called Tanganyika—over to Britain.

"In 1961, Tanganyika gained independence and, a year later, became a republic with Julius Nyerere the president. In 1964, Tanganyika and Zanzibar were united as Tanzania. Three years later Nyerere issued the Arusha Declaration, launching a program of socialism.

"Under Nyerere, cooperative programs increased primary school enrollment by 70 percent; twenty-five percent of villages had their first access to tap water. New Industries included an industrial complex, a machine-tool plant, a phosphate plant, natural gas developments and a pulp and paper mill, along with the free housing, free clinics and schools built to support the workers of these industries. But, like projects in other emerging nations, these new ventures were financed largely by foreign aid."

She stopped reading, took a sip of her tea and watched Hami lug the hose across the garden. She wondered where he would be living, and what he would be doing had the mill not been built in Ahadi; what his future would be if it closed down. She read on:

"During the 1970s, the country received some $3 billion in funds, primarily from the International Monetary Fund. In 1982 alone, Nyerere brought $600 million into the country.

"In 1985 Ali Hassan Mwinyi, former president of Zanzibar, became president of Tanzania. He inherited billions of dollars of foreign debt, nearly half of the country's budget.

"He also inherited an obligation to countries that had invested in Tanzania and expected returns.

Anna reread the next section twice as it seemed especially pertinent:

A Tanzanian Story

"African nations have long been invaded by foreigners with a passion for converting indigenous peoples to their religions, economic systems, social structures—without attempting to understand the way of life they are disturbing.

"The result can be repression and gross mismanagement of both for-profit and non-profit organizations—"

She thought about the ramifications of European encroachment, notably the bloody Mau Mau revolution just thirty years ago against colonial rule in nearby Kenya. Mau was interpreted as *Mzungu Aenda Ulaya*: white man go back abroad. She shuddered. Did the people of Ahadi see her and Aaron as intruders?

She was interrupted by the sound of the Land Cruiser pulling up to the house. Aaron got out of the left-hand seat, and Jabari drove off.

Aaron's tie was loose around his neck, and the sleeves of his blue button-down shirt were rolled up to the elbows so that his arms shimmered with bronze hair. He appeared uneasy as he set his thick briefcase down and gave Anna a hug.

"Anna," he said. "There's been a change of plans. I tried to call you from the office, but…"

"I can guess," she said. "The phones aren't working."

"I am told that's often the case," he said, shaking his head. "Believe it or not, they're solar powered, so when there's cloud cover, the cells lose their energy because there's no electric backup."

He looked into Anna's eyes with an expression that capered between hesitancy, assertiveness and exasperation. "I realize we only just arrived here, but Eric Sikes—hopefully not deliberately—neglected to tell me that I am required at a meeting at the Ministry of Industries in Dar Es Salaam Monday morning. And afterwards there's a board meeting of the

National Development Corporation. I told Jabari to go home and pack his bag because you and I are leaving for Dar this afternoon. I'm sorry, Anna. We would have stayed in the city had I only known."

"You mean you're actually taking the afternoon off?"

He laughed. "I've talked to all the managers and need some time to digest what they've said. I don't want to be forced into making any decisions until I can think more about what's going on." His eyes turned somber. "And I also need to hear what they say at the ministry."

"Can't we wait until the morning? It's a long, hard eight-hour trip to the coast. And what if it's pouring rain?"

"We have a lot to do in Dar," he said. "We need to stock up on staples and find a whole lot of household goods. Besides," he added, cocking his head and squinting down at her, "The sky is clear, and I have a surprise for you."

"But we won't get there until way past dark. I don't think it's safe to drive those gravel roads at night." While Anna appreciated Aaron's venturesome nature, at times she wondered if he wasn't too inclined to take risks. This was one of those times.

"Like I said, I have a surprise for you." He kissed her on the forehead. "And we won't be driving past dark. Besides, I need to try to see a manager at the Tanzanian National Bank before they shut down tomorrow for the weekend. We wouldn't make it in time if we leave in the morning."

He took a tape measure, a pen and sheet of paper from his briefcase. "Come help me make a list of everything we need. Then we'll measure the windows for curtains," he said.

But as soon as they stepped into the kitchen to start the list, Aaron's frustration appeared to mount. He knocked his fist on the countertop. Anna reached out to hold her hand

71

over his. "Tell me what's happening," she said.

Aaron leaned back against a cabinet and stared at the ceiling. Finally, he looked at her. "It's worse than I imagined, Anna. We've got huge problems—money problems, supply problems, transportation problems, personnel problems and undoubtedly a lot more problems I don't know about yet. Before we can decide on a course of action, I need to find out how much support we really have from the government—how badly they want this project of theirs to succeed. We can't make it work without a serious infusion of money, money the government may not even have."

"You'll get the answers you need. And you'll make the right decisions. You always have."

He draped his arm around her shoulder. "I hope you're right," he said.

"You know I'm *always* right," she said. He rewarded her with the hint of a smile.

As Anna packed to return to Dar Es Salaam, she thought about what Aaron was going through. If he was to keep this project alive, the government, deeply in debt, needed to supply him with coal, electricity, spare parts, vehicles, repairs, imported oil; with money for salaries, medicine, housing. And yet she believed in him—almost to the point of believing he could pull off this miracle as he had pulled off so many others in the past. She only wished they weren't leaving so late in the day to travel the long distance. She checked the sky again from the bedroom window. No clouds to be seen. And Aaron said they wouldn't be driving after dark. She'd have to trust him. She wouldn't probe but would let him keep his surprise a secret.

CHAPTER NINE: IT TAKES A WARTHOG

Jabari arrived at eleven o'clock and knocked on the door. He was wearing a clean white short-sleeve shirt and pressed khaki pants. Since his clipped hair was beginning to recede, his forehead was broad, as was his thoughtful smile. His face was smoothly shaven, except for a carefully trimmed mustache.

"I hope I am not coming too soon," he said. "I can wait in the car until you are ready."

Anna told him that they were just finishing packing, and he could wait inside or on the patio if he wished.

She cut up a pineapple, a cucumber, the remaining carrots from the basket and poured the last of the milk in Simba's bowl. Then she washed out the bottle with boiled water and filled it with ice and filtered water so they would have both food and drink for the road. She had no idea what to do with the stew, which needed several more hours of cooking. She suspected Hami was a Muslim and wouldn't eat it because of the wine. It wouldn't last, uncovered, in the fridge. She decided to drop it off for the Barnetts on the way out of town.

When she took the bowl of milk outside, she found Jabari on the porch rocker, quietly stroking Simba. She was purring in his lap. Anna smiled at the two of them and knew she had already begun to form a liking to both Jabari and this feisty little stray. She hoped that, before too long, the cat would want to sit in her lap, too.

She called to Hami who was still weeding along the back hedge. She told him he could pick any ripe vegetables from the garden. She also asked him to check the *paca's* dish each morning and afternoon.

"The *paca*—her name is Simba—she likes milk," Anna said

"She is *njaa* like *simba*," he said.

"*Njaa?*"

Hami quickly raised his hand to his mouth, as if eating voraciously. Anna laughed. "*Njaa*. Hungry. Always hungry. Like a lion."

"Yes, Mama. Hungry." He smiled warmly. "Your Swahili is better already."

She asked Hami if he could obtain some milk. When he nodded, she pulled from her pocket two 1,000-shilling notes—the equivalent of a little over four U.S. dollars—and asked him if that was enough to cover the cost.

"Yes, Mama, and I will care for Simba, the *paca*," he said.

She asked him if there was anything he needed for the garden, and he told her in gestures and words that a trowel and clippers went missing before the Sikes left, and there was only a small amount of fertilizer remaining. She told him she would try to find replacements in Dar.

"*Asante sana,* mama. *Safari njema.*"

She understood that he had just wished her a safe journey.

§§§

They took a lunch break at the side of the road above a bend in the Ruaha river. Below, two women were rubbing children's shorts and shirts against smooth stones in a rocky outcrop. A teenage girl was bent over a broad stretch of purple and blue cloth she was rinsing in the water. Half a dozen school-age children splashed in the shallows, and a couple of toddlers chased each other around the adjacent sandbar. Strips of vivid screen-printed *kangas*—a mixture of images in crimson, yellow, orange, indigo, turquoise—were draped across the outcrop to dry. With all the color and patterns spread out below her, Anna regretted that she still had black and white film in her camera.

As they continued down the highway, Anna stretched out on the back seat. Suddenly Jabari turned down a narrow dirt road off the left side of the highway. Anna sat up. "Jabari, where are you going?" she asked. She looked at Aaron. He smiled back at her. "I told you I had a surprise."

Ahead she saw a sign for the Mikumi National Park gate.

"Oh, Aaron. Does this mean we can actually stay here overnight?"

"Yes," he said. "And we're going to find some giraffes and elephants to photograph. Maybe even a few lions."

At the mention of the lions, Jabari gave Aaron a startled look before slowing to a stop at the gate. Aaron got out and, in a few minutes, returned to the car. He handed Jabari the park pass and said they would have two adjacent lodge huts for the night. Anna was thrilled, even more so when they passed a pair of giraffes craning their necks around the top of a Borassus palm.

Jabari stopped the car. Anna took her last two black and white pictures, rewound the cartridge and quickly loaded 400-speed color film. She attached the motor winder as the giraffes gazed at them, their legs splayed out, unmoving, their enormous eyelashes unblinking. Anna held her breath and pressed the button: *whirr, whirr, zoom out, whirr.*

At the lodge they got their keys and directions to the game trails. Aaron climbed on top of the Land Cruiser, hoisted Anna up behind him, and they took off with an hour to tour before sunset. Jabari drove slowly, evidently doing his best to find smooth ground, but the road was rough and uneven. Aaron and Anna grabbed the top luggage rail and each other.

They skirted the hippo pool, watching the huge animals snort, roll, splash through the water and waddle ashore. One raced across the grass at a pace that belied his size, halted and finally opened his jaws in a giant yawn. Anna's camera lens was aimed right down his throat.

As they turned toward the Rubaka Plain, the road roughened, and Aaron yelled down to Jabari to stop. Aaron and Anna climbed down and got inside the Land Cruiser. They were strapped into their seats just as a pair of elephants turned the corner and meandered down the road approaching them. The larger elephant stopped, lifted its trunk and snapped a large branch off an Acacia tree. Jabari backed up—quickly—and slipped into a turnaround to let the elephants pass.

Anna knew she was going through precious film on shots that might become nothing more than scrapbook memories unless she was lucky enough to have captured a good image or two. But she couldn't refrain from photographing the spectacular show they were watching—giraffes, elephants, baboons, hippos and zebras. She thought maybe the picture looking straight into the hippo's mouth would be worth something, but she wasn't counting on it.

As the sun began to fade, Jabari parked the Land Cruiser in front of their cabins. He pulled out the suitcases and Aaron's briefcase. "I'll take those," Aaron said. "You can clean up and meet us here in an hour."

Jabari looked worried and didn't move. Aaron handed him his bag and spoke to him again: "One hour—meet here for dinner. Okay?"

An hour later, after they had a meager shower and changed clothes, Aaron and Anna left the hut to find Jabari pacing back and forth in front of his door. He still looked concerned. They motioned to him to come with them to the lodge, and he followed closely behind them.

They climbed the stairs to the dining room, and, when the waiter arrived, Aaron ordered a scotch for himself and a vodka tonic for Anna. He asked Jabari if he'd like a drink, but Jabari shook his head. Each of them passed up the zebra steak in favor of broiled chicken.

While Aaron and Anna sipped their drinks, Jabari still seemed uncomfortable. He looked around the room at the few patrons—mostly white—then focused on the smooth red tablecloth.

"We aren't going anywhere tonight, Jabari, and it's nearly two weeks before Ramadan," Aaron said. "You told me in the car yesterday that your faith does not keep you from enjoying an evening beer when there is one available. I don't want to influence you, but one is available."

Jabari smiled. "Yes, sir. I would like a Tusker very much."

Aaron motioned to the waiter and ordered the beer. As they ate, Jabari began to talk. "I have never been inside a park like this before, sir," he said. "It's a new experience for me." He took a quick sip of his drink and, without putting down the glass, looked around the room. "Never have I eaten in such a place," he said.

"But Jabari," Anna said, "I am sure you drove other expatriates to Dar, and they stopped here from time to time, did they not?"

"Oh, yes, Mama, *wazungu* came here often. He carefully placed the beer on the table and rubbed his thumb around the rim. Without looking up, he continued, "But I stayed in the

77

village just outside the gate.

"Jabari," Anna said, "people travel from all over the world to see the game parks in Kenya and Tanzania. But you never once came here to see the giraffes, the elephants, the lions?"

"I have been working eight years now for TPM, and, Mama, it is true. I have only seen one lion in that whole time. He came quickly from the bush on the road where we were driving today."

Jabari hesitated, looked at Aaron and continued. "That lion was roaring, and seemed very fierce," he said. "I would not like him at my door tonight."

Aaron assured him that no lion would harm him tonight if he locked his door.

"Long before I came to Ahadi," Jabari said, "I heard that there were lions in the valley, and they passed by the tents where men lived. Those men built the first houses for work-ers who came to build the mill. One man was killed, only his bones remaining." He shivered, shook his head, continued: "But I have not heard anyone say a lion or a leopard or even a gazelle has passed through since."

Anna wondered how many of his countrymen had ever seen what they saw that day, but it was a question she felt she could answer with certainty: damn few. While there was no apartheid in Tanzania, it had only taken her a few days to understand how pervasive poverty was, and how most peo-ple were limited to survival tasks—growing food, obtaining water, tending to children. She wondered how the country might have developed had there been no colonists who felt it was their right to control dissimilar people in distant lands.

Nelson Mandela had been released from prison just a few months before, and Namibia had just become independent from South Africa. She wondered if apartheid would really end, if blacks in South Africa would stop warring on each other and have opportunities never available before, and what effect it would have, if any, on other African nations.

In ten years they would enter the 21st century. She imagined Europe and America would experience technological leaps which, like those in the past, would radically impact families, communities, relationships. She wondered what effect those changes would bring to East Africa: if women would still scrub clothes against rocks in a stream, still carry on their heads jugs of water and sticks for the cooking fire. She wondered if the night sky would still be dark enough for a boundless display of stars.

§§§

After dinner, Aaron and Anna switched on their flashlights to find their way to the cabins. Jabari followed close behind. Two enormous hawk-like birds swooped through the parking lot. One dove to the ground, and they beamed their lights toward it as it grabbed a small, furry animal in its beak. The animal let out a piercing shriek. They all stopped, hardly breathing, until the birds flew off and the noise faded. Anna shivered, realizing what she had just seen was the way of the natural world, animals preying on smaller animals. It was common, yet still terrifying to behold. She handed Jabari her flashlight. He thanked her and hurried toward his hut, the yellow beam bobbing through the darkness.

In the morning, Aaron and Anna were just ordering breakfast at a window table overlooking the Mkata Plain when Jabari arrived and, with only the slightest hesitation, asked if it was okay to join them. They welcomed him and ordered the English breakfast: toast, poached eggs, grilled tomatoes and orange juice.

"The monkeys running across our roof kept me awake," Aaron said.

"Was it just monkeys? They sounded so big!" Jabari said.

"They were big monkeys," Aaron said. "Some were quite big. But not as big as that." Aaron pointed to a lioness moving through the sisal below. The grasses rippled with each smooth step she took. Soon the grasses behind her moved, and a large male appeared. His mane was full, the fringes black, and his powerful legs stretched with each long, commanding stride. He turned his head left then right, never breaking his pace.

"Jabari," Aaron teased. "Are you afraid of that lion?"

"Oh, yes sir. Very afraid."

"Look there," Arron whispered. Peeking out from a gap in a thicket of tall reeds three hundred yards ahead of the lioness were two lion cubs, the same color as the foliage that nearly concealed them. They were huddled close to each other, looking intently toward the lodge. Suddenly they perked up their ears, sprang up and turned around, waiting for the lioness to approach them.

Anna knew that, photographing through the restaurant window with her short lens, she wouldn't get anything worth keeping, but she kept clicking away as the lioness, the lion and the cubs moved forward out of the sisal toward the lodge. Even as they made a sudden turn and headed down a trail leading into the park, she kept taking pictures. She quickly slipped her last color cartridge into the camera and realized she'd have to figure out where to find more film in Dar Es Salaam.

Aaron turned to Jabari. "I don't think you're afraid of those two little lions."

"No, sir," he said. "They are only *watoto*."

"Do you have children?" Anna asked.

He beamed. "I have three *watoto*," he said, "a daughter, Johani, now six, and twin boys, two years her senior."

When Aaron ordered another cup of coffee, Anna excused herself. She went into the small gift shop where she selected a wildlife coloring book and small box of crayons for Jabari's daughter, Johani, and, for each of the twins, a red tee-shirt screened with the face of a roaring lion, its mane ruffed out and the teeth prominent, sharp. Then she noticed a similar lion screened onto a yellow tee-shirt. It would fit Jabari. She added it to the pile.

When she returned to the table, Jabari opened the bag and looked intently at every picture in the coloring book. He called each animal by their Swahili name: *chui, tembo, twiga, simba, nyani, kiboko, punda milia*. Anna responded with the English names: leopard, elephant, giraffe, lion, baboon, hippo, zebra. They repeated the names in both languages and continued to test each other until they had all of them right. Jabari took the blue crayon from the box and drew the Land Cruiser facing the elephant.

Aaron looked closely at the picture. "You are an artist, Jabari," he said.

Jabari laughed. "I am a driver. Johani will become an artist with this book."

Then Jabari pulled out the shirts. He held the yellow shirt up to his chest. "My sons and I are now as *mkali* as *simba*," he said. He made a fierce face, laughed, then carefully folded the shirts and put them back in the bag.

"Thank you, Mama GM," he said. "We are lucky to have these gifts from you."

They spent an hour driving through the park, spotted some kudu, a herd of zebra, more giraffes. Two warthogs dashed by at an astonishing speed then stopped abruptly and knelt to root in the soil. Their heads were large, flat, and the larger one—obviously a male from his testicles—had long bumps protruding above his small, skin-shrouded eyes and another set of bumps behind the curved tusks extending from his snout. Smaller, sharper tusks jutted up against the larger ones. A single tuft of scraggly red hair grew from his flat head, and a thin reddish mane flopped across his scarred and wrinkled back. His tail was shabby, skinny.

The smaller warthog approached the male, then rubbed up against him. She leaned into his flank. When Anna took a picture of the two warthogs, she felt as if she could see affection in their eyes. She turned and took Aaron's picture, capturing tenderness in his eyes as well.

"It takes a warthog to love a warthog," Aaron said. Anna laughed.

"I wonder how they would fare in Vermont," he added.

"Don't take that thought an inch further," Anna said. They both laughed.

Two other females appeared, and behind them a pack of piglets. The male rose and headed off toward a dried-up riverbed. The females and piglets raced after him.

"I think he is a lucky *nguruwe* tonight," Jabari said.

§§§

After the warthogs crossed the muddy riverbed and disappeared into the grasslands beyond, a white bird emerged from the reeds—a stork with a pure black saddle, bright red legs and a long bright red and black-striped bill capped by a brilliant yellow beak wattle. The stork's eyes were a dazzling orange. Anna was so spellbound by this astonishing creature that she stared at it for a full minute before thinking to take a picture. When she raised her camera, the stork lifted its magnificent wings, surprisingly black and broadly edged in white. It strained to fly, and she caught it with the last frame on her last roll of film.

As they left the park, Anna hoped that she had captured the animals' magnificence. Here they ranged through some three thousand kilometers of terrain which included rivers, savannahs and mountains. She hoped that her pictures would appear as if nobody was behind the camera; nobody intruding on land that, she believed, rightfully belonged to them.

A Tanzanian Story

CHAPTER TEN: THE SIP-SIP CAFÉ

*F*our hours and 300 kilometers later they entered the city and rolled down the windows to the rush of dense heat and the smell of saltwater. Oyster Bay had no vacancies, so they ended up at the large Kilimanjaro Hotel overlooking the ships in Dar Es Salaam bay, a protected harbor off the brilliant turquoise Indian Ocean. Their room was decorated in exaggerated luxury: walls painted burgundy, a plush burgundy bedspread and matching slipcovers on the chairs.

While Anna settled in, Jabari and Aaron took off for the Bank of Tanzania. They returned in less than an hour. "The director in charge of our project was on holiday," Aaron said, "but all is not lost. I have an appointment to see him Tuesday morning." He smiled at Anna, a teasing twinkle in his eyes. "So let's assume our meeting will be favorable and tomorrow morning we'll start shopping for a long stay in Ahadi."

Jabari arrived early on Saturday and led them to shops to hunt down the goods on their list. An Indian-owned food store was nearly empty—no bread, no meat, a smattering of canned vegetables, but tucked in a row of small shops nearby was a hardware store, roofed with sheets of rusted tin. Jabari honked his way into a parking spot, scattering a dozen people, two of them pushing hand carts, one straddling a bike. He just missed a couple of chickens pecking in the dust. Inside they found a wealth of goods: spackle for the walls, full-size ice cube trays, a plug-in travel cooler, cooking pots, two cookie sheets, even a griddle. In the back room were the garden tools and fertilizer Hami requested—and a small push lawnmower. Anna looked up at Aaron. "What do you think?"

"I think you have just made a friend for life."

Jabari made inquiries of several people in the street, then led Anna and Aaron to an alley where they found a tailor and his young assistant in an open market stall sitting at manual sewing machines set on a red dirt floor. They were pushing the pedals with their bare feet. The tailor was sewing a beltloop into a pair of red trousers, and the boy beside him was hemming an embroidered white kaftan. They both wore crocheted Kufi skullcaps, gray hair curling below the tailor's cap, and a frayed blue woven prayer rug lay between them. Jabari greeted the tailor who rose and greeted each of them in turn.

Jabari and the tailor spoke for some time, with many nods and gestures. Finally, the tailor bowed to Aaron, then Anna, and slipped out behind the stall. Jabari explained that he had gone to get samples of cloth for curtains. When he returned some ten minutes later, he was carrying on his head a foam pillow and eight bolts of cotton cloth, all in shades of green. "Only green?" Anna asked.

Jabari conferred again with the tailor. "Only these, Mama," he said. Anna selected the softest color, a light mint green. Aaron gave him a sheet of paper with the dimensions and pulled a curtain hook from his pocket. The tailor assured them that he had enough for all the windows as well as slip-covers for the couch.

"But we need them by Tuesday," Aaron said. The tailor laughed. "Of course." He looked at the boy. "*Jumanni*," he said. The boy nodded, "*Jumanni*," the tailor repeated and pointed to one o'clock on his large, bright gold watch.

After the tailor wrote up a ticket and requested a down

payment, Aaron handed him a thick stack of Tanzanian shilling notes. The tailor turned to face the back wall of the stall and carefully counted out the notes, then turned back to Aaron, smiling broadly. For the first time, Anna noticed a gold tooth glinting behind two missing incisors. She wondered if the tailor would still be in the stall when they returned on Tuesday.

Back at the hotel entrance, Aaron pulled 5,000 shillings from his pocket and told Jabari he was free to go. "I'll park the car, and we'll see you at 8:30 Monday morning." Jabari thanked him, jumped from the car and rushed off to the bus stop.

Aaron opened his wallet and peered inside. Besides a couple of blank checks from the Vermont National Bank, there were only six bills left: three crumpled blue hundred-shilling notes and three dirty, pink 50s. "I'll be back in half an hour," he said. "Time to go see my soon-to-be friend, Jerry."

"How far are you going to drive?" Anna asked.

"To that empty parking spot, two rows back," he said.

"And that will take half an hour?"

"Jerry is just across the street."

Anna then noticed the sign: Jerry's Liquor Store. "And you're going to buy a bottle of scotch with 450 shillings?"

He grinned. "It's magic! See you in the room."

Indeed, in half an hour, Aaron returned with a fifth of Johnnie Walker Red and his wallet replenished with 1,000-shilling notes and one less blank check.

"Why didn't you just go to the bank?" Anna asked.

"The exchange rate is much more favorable at Jerry's," he said.

"How did you know that?"

"Whether he asks the question or not, one of the first things a foreign businessman learns in a new country is where to go for a favorable rate of exchange."

"What else does he learn?" Anna asked.

"The nearest place to buy a bottle of scotch."

§§§

On Monday morning, Aaron and Anna swallowed their weekly malaria pills, then filled up on pastries, fresh pineapple and papaya at the hotel breakfast buffet before he was to take off for the ministry. Just as they were leaving, Ryder McGowan, the pulp-mill manager, showed up in the buffet line. They hadn't seen him at the hotel, and he appeared to be taking advantage of a free breakfast. Aaron said he wondered why Ryder was even in town and asked Anna to wait while he talked to him.

In the elevator going upstairs, Aaron told Anna that McGowan mumbled something to him about coming to town to renew his visa. "I'll check it out fully when we return," he said. "And, no, he's not staying here, but feels it's his right to have a decent free breakfast."

Anna recognized the dismay, the frustration in Aaron's eyes. She took his hand and squeezed it. He didn't return the squeeze. "I don't know, Anna. I just don't get it. Where is that man's sense of responsibility?"

After Jabari dropped Aaron off at the ministry, he and Anna shopped for the rest of the morning and ended up parked outside a sagging wooden store with a small sign on the post: *Photo Studio*. The proprietor, a heavy-set, gray-haired Indian man, was asleep in a chair. Jabari woke him up, and Anna sifted through his box of assorted film and pulled out three boxes of Ilford 400-speed black and white plus two rolls of Fuji color film, all dated five years ago. She hoped the film would still print, and that their air shipment would arrive soon with more film and some rudimentary darkroom equipment.

On their way back to the Kilimanjaro, as Anna absorbed the energy emanating from the streets—the variety of skin tones, mixture of urgent and laughing voices, the despondent and hopeful faces—she realized that, while she had believed she was here only because Aaron was here, there was more to it. Like Aaron, she longed to know what lay beyond the mountains of Vermont. She also wanted to know what she was meant to do with what she learned.

§§§

Aaron was late getting back to the hotel. Anna started to read Steve's treatise. When her anxiety about Aaron's absence rose, she began to pace the room. She went to the window, looked out over the harbor, returned to the chair, picked up the book she'd bought that morning, *The Africans*, by David Lamb. She put it down, checked her watch again and again. She rode the elevator down to the lobby, walked through the front door intending to take some pictures of the carvers set up on the nearby lawn. But when she looked through the lens, instead of seeing interesting faces, skillful hands at work, images of Aaron raced through her mind like a stuttering reel of movie film. What if, in this mysterious, busy city, where they knew no one, he was in danger? What if Jabari had wrecked the car? What if the meeting hadn't gone well; if he'd wandered into some dimly lit bar? What if he was gazing at a beautiful, flirtatious blonde? She returned to the room.

At six thirty, the key turned in the lock, and Aaron walked in smiling and apologizing for the last meeting running late. Anna's concerns, which seemed so real, so rational only a

89

few moments before, quickly vanished.

Aaron was cautiously optimistic. He said that the Minister of Industries enthusiastically introduced him to all the key personnel. The board meeting was good, and his presence may have quelled—at least for now—any plan to change to another management firm.

He slipped his jacket over the back of the desk chair, removed his tie and tossed it on the dresser, then loosened his shirt collar. He went to the closet, took from his suitcase the new bottle of scotch and a half-filled bottle of Mouton Cadet, then went to the bathroom for two glasses. He filled Anna's half way up with wine and poured an inch of scotch in his. He added two inches of water to the scotch and stirred it with his finger.

Anna told him to close his eyes and hold out his drink. She took a handful of ice cubes from the cooler they'd bought the day before and plopped them into his glass.

"How in God's name? Woman, you never cease to amaze me."

"You can thank Jabari." Anna sat down on the foot of the bed. "He drove me down a strip of dirt connected by potholes. There were the usual tin-roofed buildings and a crush of people. Goat meat was roasting in tin drums, and electric wires were drooping from poles. The electric wires gave me hope. He ran into a place called the Sip-Sip Café. I looked inside. It was a dark room with stools around a Formica counter and curtains across the rear, an ominous kind of place. I couldn't imagine why Jabari took me there, but he came right back out and led me to the stall out front to buy a plastic bucket, then he went back into the café and emerged with the bucket full of ice. He is amazing!"

"I think the café also has sleeping rooms," Anna said.

"It's owned by a brother-in-law or a brother-in-law's cousin or aunt. Some relation. It might be where Jabari stays when he is in Dar. I don't have a good feeling about it."

Aaron handed Anna the wine, took a swallow of his drink and sat down beside her. His kiss was cold from the ice and smelled like scotch, which always reminded Anna of the odor of dying moss. He raised his glass: "To Jabari!"

Then his eyes turned contemplative. "Those small restaurants with sleeping rooms can be dangerous places for truckers and drivers," he said. "The reason AIDS has spread across all the major African highways is because of the unprotected sex between drivers and the women who frequent cheap hotels."

"Surely Jabari..."

"We can only hope," he said. "But he's away from home a good deal of the time, and, as you know, this is a polygamous nation."

They were both quiet for a few moments. Anna thought about all the long trips Aaron had made, weeks away from home, but she squashed the thought before it led her down a path she didn't want to follow. "Tell me about your meeting," she said.

"The whole idea," he began, "is to produce enough newsprint and sack Kraft paper to meet Tanzania's needs and improve the balance of trade by selling the excess to other East African countries. But we're dependent on imports for too many essentials. The World Bank and IMF should have figured that out before funding the project."

He started to raise his glass again but stopped. "First off, they should have realized that the country doesn't produce enough coal to power our boiler, much less supply every other business here which depends on coal. And getting coal delivered is another problem due to the unpaved roads and the damage they do to vehicles. The Chinese-built coal company doesn't have enough tires to keep their Fiat trucks rolling. Since the trucks were bought with Italian aid, they're bound by contract to use Italian replacement parts. If their front-end loader worked, they might be able to pile some coal onto a railroad car for delivery, but—"

Aaron finally took another swallow of his drink and wiped his mouth with his hand. He got up and looked out the window at the backlog of ships in the harbor. "So much promise," he said. "So little money." He turned back toward Anna. "Tanesco is already threatening to cut the electricity to the mill and the township. And we're so far behind with payments to Agip, I don't know how long they'll deliver the diesel it takes to keep the generator going."

His eyes softened briefly, then turned resolute again. "Our first job is to figure out how to make the mill run. Then we need to make it run as efficiently as possible. After that, we'll see how much shortfall there really is, and how—if— the government can help us reduce that gap."

He paused, looked out the window again, then continued. "Most people in developed nations go through life comfortably advancing in their jobs, floor by floor. They don't want to jump off the escalator. Some people accept jobs in less-developed countries because they feel their escalator at home has stopped moving up. Or they're attracted to the overseas perks, like travel allowances and household help, more money, tax breaks. And when those expats arrive, they find themselves in positions they've only dreamt of at home. They're better educated, more sophisticated, richer by far than most of their employees."

"They've had more advantages," Anna said. "So they

imagine themselves superior to everyone else."

Aaron turned back to her. "Yes. You nailed it. I think we can make some improvements, but we can't do it alone. The mill workers will have to want to make it happen. The sad part is, no matter how much we want to, no matter how hard we try, we won't be able to solve many of the problems we'll encounter."

"But maybe we can solve some of them," Anna said.

Aaron joined her on the bed, pulled her toward him, stroked her ear with his tongue. "We sure as hell are going to try," he whispered.

A Tanzanian Story

CHAPTER ELEVEN: WHERE IS SIMBA?

*W*ednesday morning Jabari pulled up to the hotel entrance at 8:00. They checked out and loaded the curtains and pillows, the lawnmower, stacks of groceries and the cooler into the Land Cruiser.

Outside of Morogoro, they stopped to look at baskets being sold by a tall Maasai woman, a bright scarlet cloth tied like a toga at her shoulder. Strands of blue, red and purple beads draped from her hennaed hair, from her elongated ears and neck. The lidded baskets, stacked by the roadside, were as large as hampers, woven of natural sisal and decorated with stripes dyed chartreuse, yellow and mauve.

"*Jambo*," the woman said, welcoming them. She smiled, her teeth large and bright. The price for a basket was 3,000 shillings, hardly enough, it seemed to Anna, to cover the cost of the material. Anna selected three. Jabari shook his head at the price and jumped in to bargain for them. He talked quickly, listened, frowned, walked away, returned, jested with the woman, conferred with Anna, shook his head, laughed, then finally nodded.

Jabari picked up the three baskets Anna had selected. "These are very fine, Mama," he said. "I think 6,000 shillings is a fair price for all three."

Anna imagined the baskets in her house in Vermont—one by the fireplace, one beside the bookcase, one in the corner next to the desk.

As they pulled away, two young men close in age, close enough in appearance to be brothers, emerged on the roadside as if materializing from the dust. Their spines were straight, hennaed hair closely cut. Like the basket seller, they were dressed in scarlet cloths knotted at their shoulders. They, too, were draped in beads. They carried spears—hewn sticks with long, slender steel blades wedged into the ends. They waved their spears at the car. Jabari slowed down.

Anna wanted nothing more at this moment than to photograph these beautiful young men. "Oh, Jabari, do you think I could take their picture?" she asked.

He stopped the car. "Usually they will refuse," he said, "but I will try."

He approached the two men and, again, spoke quickly, listened, laughed then finally nodded. He returned to the car. "It's okay, Mama. But just for one minute."

As Anna grabbed her camera, the two Maasai stood in the tall grass facing the car, arms poised as if to throw their spears. Their faces were somber. In the distance behind them was a line of feathery trees, and, farther away, against the broad horizon, loomed a low range of indigo blue mountains, several shades darker than the clouds accumulating in the sky.

With Tri-X 400 speed black and white film loaded in the Canon, Anna realized she'd have to shoot for drama rather than for the brilliant array of color in the Maasai's clothing and the landscape beyond. She stooped, zoomed in the lens and photographed one of the Maasai from the waist up, his spear in the air, high above the line of mountains.

All the while, Aaron and Jabari were engaging the Maasai in conversation, Aaron speaking English and Jabari translating. The two men replied in Swahili but didn't break their serious pose.

"Jabari," Anna asked, "Do you think you can get them to

face each other?"

After Jabari spoke to them, the young man on the right turned, and, again, they lifted their spears. Anna stood on the running board to gain some height, zoomed out and took a quick shot of the two of them, their profiles nearly matching, their spears raised to the same height.

Aaron whispered something to Jabari who laughed and spoke to the two men. They also began to laugh. Anna took a final shot, and Aaron handed them each some shilling notes from his wallet.

After they got into the car, Anna asked Jabari how he convinced them to let her take the pictures.

"I asked them if they would sell me a goat for Ramadan. They said they had no goat." He smiled. "If they had a goat to sell, it would have been a problem. So then I asked if you could take their picture. They couldn't refuse me twice."

Although Anna didn't understand the logic, she was grateful to Jabari for negotiating—twice—on her behalf. She was also glad there was no goat riding in the back of the Land Cruiser.

§§§

Because Anna had promised to pick up the food baskets, they skirted the town of Iringa and detoured up a steep gradient to Catherine Dennison's farm. Neat rows of vegetables grew near the house, a rambling Tudor tucked into a hillside. Below, all the way down to the highway, was fenced-in land. A young man herded a flock of sheep through one of the gates. Cows grazed across an adjoining meadow.

A young girl greeted them at the door and motioned them into the parlor where two oversized gray horsehair sofas and a sideboard with cornucopias carved into the door panels appeared to have materialized from Victorian London.

The girl waited just outside the parlor until Mrs. Dennison emerged from upstairs and told her to fetch rock cakes and tea. The scones the girl brought were studded with dried pineapple and, indeed, hard as rocks, and the English tea was robust and bitter. Mrs. Dennison, tall and stately, appeared just as robust as the tea, but in no way bitter.

She told them that her husband's family settled in Tanzania in the late 1800s, and she met him in the 1950s when he was sent back to England for schooling. "My family thought I was batty when I actually agreed to marry Michael and come out here. They were certain I'd be devoured by a lion or scalped by a native."

She chuckled, refilled her flowered teacup from the dainty matching porcelain pot beside her and looked at Aaron then Anna with a raised eyebrow to ask if they wanted a refill. Both Aaron and Anna shook their heads.

"But I believe I was meant to be here," Mrs. Dennison said. She tucked a wisp of white hair behind her ear and raised her blue half-moon eyes which caught the light from the far window. She smiled while looking out over the farm. "Where else would I be allowed to manage 180 hectares and twelve employees?"

She said it had been fourteen years since her husband died from what she called an undiagnosed tropical disease, fourteen years of managing the farm.

"And you did it all alone?" Anna asked.

"No, no," she said. "Not me. My employees run the farm. They also turned my children into respectable adults. I just pay the overseer who manages the employees and takes care of the bills."

Anna was certain that Mrs. Dennison gave herself far less credit than she deserved.

§§§

As they headed toward Ahadi, Anna stretched out on the back seat of the Land Cruiser, a stack of curtains for a pillow. She looked out of the window at clouds floating between treetops and thought of the women she had met during this first week. She was disappointed that, other than the Maasai basket seller, none of them were Tanzanian.

First, she thought of the steadfast Catherine Dennison, who appeared to have admirably persisted beyond the land-grabbing, gin-drinking, horse-racing, spouse-swapping, big-game-stalking colonists depicted by Ernest Hemingway and Karen Blixen. Mrs. Dennison seemed truly at home in Africa, and she wondered if, some day, she might feel the same way.

Then she considered Tallulah and wondered why she left Eureka Creek; what her church's outpost mission would mean to her when her assignment was over. She wondered if Tallulah would feel that she had done her part, or if there was more she had wanted to do.

She imagined Priscilla Fuller returning to Arkansas, amusing her bridge group with stories of the inconveniences she'd endured in Africa. Anna assumed that Priscilla had never faced greater hardships, so she could appreciate, if not condone, her attitude.

She still couldn't fathom Glenna Sikes.

But then there was Becky Barnett. Anna had only seen her that night at dinner, but Becky seemed to have found a place for herself in Ahadi. She volunteered at the school, became involved with the villagers. Anna felt she had a good deal to learn from Becky. She'd ask Jabari to stop by the Barnett's house on his way home tonight and leave word for Becky to stop by if she could in the morning.

A faint mist arose across the escarpment as they reached the outskirts of Ahadi. Here and there Anna spotted men wearing knit caps, though the temperature hovered in the low seventies.

She expected to find Simba at the back door and Hami in the garden. Neither one appeared when she called. But under a rock on the patio table was a strip of paper torn from a fertilizer bag. She turned it over to find a long, penciled note written in Swahili and signed Hami.

Jabari finished stacking the last of the curtains on the dining room table, and Anna asked him to translate the note. Aaron dropped a box of groceries in the kitchen and joined them to listen.

"Hami says he is very sorry, Mama, that he cannot write well in English, but he wants you to understand that he became sick with Tanzanian flu. Babu Bungara has given him a very good potion, so he expects to be back at work tomorrow."

"What is Tanzanian flu?" Anna asked.

"It is the very same thing as malaria, Mama."

"Tell me about Babu Bungara," Aaron said.

"He is a very powerful healer, sir. I have been to him myself three times."

Jabari waved his hand in a gesture that took in the whole room. "In his hut on the road beyond the market are more than a hundred bottles of medicine he gathers from the forest during the dry season when the moon is big. His father was also a famous healer. And I think his grandfather, too."

Jabari studied Aaron's questioning eyes. "Bungara is now growing old, a grandfather as well," he said. "He is beginning to teach his grandson all that he knows."

"Do many people in the village go to Babu Bungara

when they are sick?"

"Yes, many people. He is a very fine doctor."

"Jabari, tell me one thing," Aaron said. "We have a legitimate medical doctor on staff, plus two nurses. It costs employees nothing to use these facilities. How is it that Babu Bungara has any business at all?"

Jabari appeared to choose his words carefully. "It is tradition," he said. "Our ancestors even knew such men who give us what is good for the body and kill the bad juju that has entered here." He put his hand over his heart.

"But," he added, "if Babu feels he cannot help us, he will suggest we see the doctor."

"Is the doctor not trusted?" Aaron asked.

Jabari hesitated before replying: "Not so much. We have experienced some problems, sir."

Aaron appeared to ponder Jabari's answer. "What...," he began to ask. "Never mind," he said and simply nodded.

"There is more to this letter," Jabari said. He read on and told them that, when Hami was waiting to see Babu Bungara, Samwell, his grandson, said a witch doctor had passed through the market that very morning. "This man, who called himself only Mtu—the Swahili word for man— was willing to pay well for a cat. The grandson had heard of a certain witch doctor who would chew off a cat's head to cast a favorable spell for a politician or rich businessman. Perhaps this Mtu is that very man."

Anna was revolted at the thought of someone clamping their teeth around the neck of a cat; tearing off its head. And she was even more anxious about Simba. She looked out at the garden, hoping to see the cat. Nothing moved. She listened carefully. She heard no meows, no hungry cries.

"Jabari, how does killing a cat create good juju for

101

someone? And what about Simba?"

"Don't worry. Simba is safe," Jabari said. "Many people think a cat is bad luck. Some think that evil spirits take the form of cats and killing the cat kills the spirit. Some even think that drinking a cat's blood gives them power." He shook his head. "I am not one of those people."

Jabari then translated directly from the end of the letter: "Mama, I captured Simba and took her home to make sure Mtu doesn't steal her. She is staying in my room until you return. She has food and milk. I will bring her when I return to work very soon. Your gardener, Hami Kamala."

Anna wondered if Hami might not have made more money than he was likely to ever see by handing Simba over to Mtu. She was only just getting to know Hami, but she was stunned by his integrity, his goodness, and found herself trying, without success, to hold back tears.

The next week would begin the month of Ramadan. Hami and Jabari would fast from sunrise to sunset—from Sahur to Iftar. They'd refrain from smoking, from sex. They'd read the Quran and perform acts of charity. With an earnestness that made Anna feel even more respectful of these two men, Jabari had told her that Allah had favored him with a good job, a fine house and family, and a month of fasting was nothing in return.

§§§

The next morning, Hami returned, Simba in his arms. As Anna carried a bowl of milk to the patio, she saw a slight man dressed in white pants and a New York Mets tee-shirt speaking with Hami. They laughed and slapped hands. Clearly, they were friends.

When she went into the kitchen a few minutes later, she saw the same man wheeling a fat-tired bicycle through the gate to the servants' quarters. His features were refined, handsome; his wrists and arms firm, and his long neck solid, strong. He parked the bike against the wall and stood there, nervously rubbing his hands together. She surmised that Tobias had returned. He approached the back door, his hand outstretched to open it. She stepped back as he entered. "*Jambo*," she said.

"*Jambo*, Mama," he said, speaking just above a whisper. He gazed around the kitchen but avoided looking directly at her.

He bowed his head and scraped the toe of a pristine white Nike across the stone tiles. After a long pause he said, "Mama GM, I am Mrs. Sikes' boy, Tobias Mgomo. I have come to beg you humbly. Please. Do not be angry with me."

"Should I be angry, Tobias?"

His voice rose with anxiety. "Mama, please do not sack me."

His demeanor contradicted his solid appearance. "But Tobias, I am told that you had a new job at a hotel in Dar Es Salaam."

He shook his head, looked back down at the floor. "There is no job for me at a hotel."

He lifted his head and finally looked at her, his eyes wide open, first with expectancy, then with a tinge of fear. "Oh, please, Mama, I am praying very hard to work for you and the GM."

"As far as I know, Tobias, you do work for us."

"He nodded, bowed again, backed away, and his face broke into a wide smile.

§§§

Tobias settled earnestly into the kitchen, and he and Anna roasted peanuts, made peanut butter and peanut butter

103

cookies, mayonnaise, mustard, French dressing, potato chips, refrigerator pickles, cottage cheese, sour cream, banana bread and muffins. They marinated and ground Mrs. Dennison's lamb; stuffed eggplants and peppers; made shepherd's pie. They marinated and ground beef to make meatloaf, chili and spaghetti sauce. They nearly filled one of the freezers in the servant's quarters. The work satisfied Anna. She was pleased at what they could create from scratch; she was also pleased by Tobias' self-confidence.

They learned that a second gardener, Eva Pengo, was assigned to the GM, but the Sikes had dismissed her after a few months, so she was waiting reassignment. Jabari tracked down Eva at her parents' small wattle home outside the village. Eva, with large, hopeful eyes, a reluctant smile, was seventeen. She wore pink beads woven into braids which lay close to her scalp. Her complexion was bright, flawless, as if polished with soft chamois. Because her parents couldn't afford to send her to secondary school, she'd been working since she was fourteen. Anna hired her to work inside. The next day she promoted Tobias to cook.

Each day Eva mopped, dusted, then retreated to the first bedroom where she assiduously ironed all the clothes. Ironing was essential to kill the larvae of the tumbu, or mango fly, an insect which infected humans by laying its eggs on wet clothes left out to dry. She also ironed distinct creases into the pockets and buttonholes of Aaron's dress shirts.

Hami goaded the little lawnmower through the tough crabgrass lawn. He and Anna began to regroup the flowers in the garden to use less water when the dry season began. They designed a compost bin for the far corner, then, closer to the house, sketched in a small pond and a bench—a place to read and reflect on life. Hami named it the thinking garden.

Simba became an indoor cat and ran to the door each evening when Aaron returned from work. The household was now complete.

§§§

Anna had spent just three weeks in this vast, alluring, baffling land. She'd met missionaries and Muslims, Maasai herders, expatriates both indifferent and committed. She'd slept among lions and giraffes and learned of men who chewed off cats' heads. She'd seen a pleasure ground for the wealthy and a garbage dump which served as a playground for the poorest of the poor.

She'd seen her husband angered and determined to save what may be impossible to save. She'd seen all these things through the long lens of a visitor and now resolved to zoom in closer. She resolved to feel at home.

A Tanzanian Story

INTERMEZZO

*L*ike any village, any town, there was a distinct rhythm to Ahadi, a melody which began every morning just past dawn as the whistle sounded for the morning shift, and workers filed in to take their places at the massive, often silent, machines.

After breakfast, Tobias arrived on his fat-tired bicycle, took a shower in the servants' quarters and changed into a clean tee-shirt before entering the kitchen. Hami pulled the hose out from the shed. Eva hung wet clothes on the line.

Shortly thereafter, a dozen or so vendors approached the market with baskets of goods on their heads: charcoal, dried fish, rock salt, Omo soap powder, Kimbo shortening, fermented bamboo juice.

Drums sounded in the distance, and two hundred children, wearing blue shorts or skirts, thin white shirts, ran from home to line up by age in the school yard. They waited on bare soil, dusty or muddy, depending on the season, then entered their cement-block classrooms and stood until allowed to sit four to a row on rough benches. The chalkboards had been erased so many times the slate was worn, and the letters and numbers were faint, shadowy.

In the heat of late afternoon, men, women and older children emerged from their homes carrying hoes and water buckets to the communal *shamba* where they cared for their few rows of maize, cassava or chard.

And as the daylight faded, women gathered together on their back stoops, their faces lit by single, bare light bulbs. They talked, wove baskets, braided their daughters' hair.

Some of their husbands, men with titles, drifted into the Bwana Club to drink a Tusker or Safari Lager, or, if they were mill workers, stopped by the Mdogo Club for companionship and, perhaps, after payday, a Fanta Orange or a Coke.

All day long, well into the night, workers and family members stood at the Ahadi gate and waved at cars leaving or entering the village. "*Lifti, lifti*," they shouted. "*Lifti Tadfahali. Lifti*, please." There was no public transportation in or out; no way to get back to their village for a sister's wedding or a mother's funeral.

And each evening, Aaron returned from the mill and tried to wash down his fatigue with a Johnny Walker Red and a walk through the garden. But often, as he and Anna sat down to dinner, there was someone at the door with a problem to be solved, a check to be signed, a rumor to squelch or spread, a complaint to lodge. If the phones were working, there could be a call from Dar Es Salam or from the bankers in London or the home office in New York, a long call, which, after a quick meal, sent Aaron with a cup of coffee to his computer in the back bedroom.

The daily rhythm of Ahadi became the refrain of Anna's life. But the melody was often interspersed with phrases, sometimes full movements, played *amoroso* or *bellicose*; *capriccioso* or *obbligato*; *fortissimo, expansivo* or *dolore*.

PART TWO

Mngurumo wa Simba
The Lion Roars

April through December,1990

CHAPTER TWELVE:
RYDER MCGOWAN THUMBS A RIDE

Christopher wrote that the ice-out on the Connecticut River was massive that year, giant globes of ice churning down the river, taking trees and decks, a cow, a pickup truck. "They let me borrow a camera from the studio," he wrote, "and I taped it from our balcony, then went down to Don's place where I got incredible footage at eye level. They let me help edit it this afternoon, and it appeared on the evening news. Can you believe it? My tape made it to the evening news—and, even better—they picked up some footage in Boston! I'll convert it to VHS tomorrow and send you a copy."

Christopher closed the letter saying he hoped he'd be able to take the Mad River canoe out on Lake Fairlee in a couple of days because he was hankering for some fishing.

"P.S. The ice-out took about eight inches of soil from our bank, but no major damage. We only lost a couple of small birches. You'll see it when I send the footage."

Anna was thrilled for Christopher and knew the airing of his footage was a major boost in confidence for him. She hoped it would help propel him toward applying to graduate school to pursue his dream of becoming a producer. She also wondered if it was a mistake to leave their house in Christopher's care. Though tall and bearded with a husky man's voice, a girlfriend and a job, it really wasn't that long ago that Aaron was teaching him how to ride a bike; that Anna was teaching him to look through a camera lens.

Anna couldn't help but compare Christopher's future with those of her young household workers. As she watched Tobias, Hami and Eva repeat their mundane tasks day after day, she became determined to encourage them toward a less dreary future. She told Tobias that, if he had spare time, he could use the kitchen to bake bread to sell. She offered to tutor Hami on Monday and Wednesday afternoons so he could apply for a correspondence course to finish secondary school. He readily accepted. She asked Eva if she would like to study English. "*Ndio*, yes please, Mama," Eva said, her eyes pleading. So Anna began to give her lessons each Tuesday.

§§§

As Anna was tutoring Hami on a Monday afternoon in mid-April, Jabari and Aaron hauled in the crate containing their air shipment. Together they pried it open, left it just inside the front door and hurried back to the mill.

When the lesson was over, she reached into the crate and pulled out one of the two dozen small soccer balls she had bought at the last minute and used to fill the box. She tossed it to the first boy who passed on the road. He kicked aside his old round of cloth wrapped in string and ran down the street, hugging the little black and white ball to his chest.

Anna wished she had shipped out a hundred more.

Back at the house she took the small enlarger, safe light, packets of chemicals and photographic paper from the crate and set up a darkroom in the second bathroom. At last, she would be able to see what she had created with her camera.

When she went back down the hall to unpack the clothes and books, she heard Eva humming as she was ironing. Anna looked at the shirt she had just hung on a hanger. The creases were less noticeable. "*Nzuri,*" she said. Eva smiled brightly.

Toward the end of their next tutoring session, Anna was explaining to Hami that adding "ed" to most verbs created the past tense in English and asked him to name some examples. He caught on quickly. "Mow, mowed," he said. "That's right," Anna replied. "Rake, raked," he said. "Good!" said Anna. "Spend, spended," he said.

"Actually, no. The past tense is 'spent'." Hami laughed and scratched his head. "Hami," Anna said, "we'll tackle irregular verbs next week. You've done well today."

Anna stayed at the table on the patio, writing down a list of all the irregular verbs she could think of. "Bite, bit, the past participle, bitten. Keep, kept, kept. Write, wrote, written. Teach, taught, taught. Feel, felt, felt. Hurt, hurt, hurt." There were a lot more, and she'd never think of all of them. She needed a grammar book and would ask Christopher to send her one. "Know, knew, known."

She closed the notebook and was just entering the house when Aaron pulled up in a red Suzuki which looked a lot like the one Priscilla Fuller had been using. Jabari parked behind him in the Land Cruiser. Aaron dashed inside, waving a car key.

"Priscilla Fuller has use of a perfectly serviceable Land Cruiser and any driver of her choice," he said. "From here on out, this Suzuki, this so-called automobile, stays here as backup for us. And we may very well need it."

He handed Anna the key. "Guard this with your life."

She put the key in her pocket. "What do you mean exactly, Aaron?"

"I mean we need to make sure one vehicle is running at all times, so we have a way out if it comes to that."

"Is it coming to that?" she asked. "Are we in some kind of danger?"

"No. Nothing more than business as usual. There's always a danger, but nothing imminently threatening I don't think. Another thing, Chief Shasani, the Minister of Industries, has been known to request the GM's car for transport here and back to Dar, and he's hinting that he may visit soon, so we'll need an alternate vehicle."

"Aaron…what's going on?"

He shook his head. "It's okay, Anna. I'm just a bit bent out of shape."

"Because?"

Aaron paced the living room as he talked: "One of our five remaining Land Cruisers, the one signed over to Ryder McGowan, was found just this side of Iringa with the driver's window broken in, the tires, radio and windshield wipers stolen. Evidently, last night Ryder ran out of beer and took off on a shopping trip. When the car broke down, he left it at the roadside and thumbed a ride."

"You have to be kidding me. Ryder 'ornges' McGowan? The pulp mill manager? He thumbed a ride?"

"Well, actually, he flagged down one of our trucks heading back here and demanded that the driver turn around and take him to a bar in Iringa. The driver waited while Ryder had a couple of beers and ordered a couple to go. Then, at Ryder's insistence, he loaded two cases of Tusker in the truck. Ryder drank his way back up the mountain."

Aaron waved his hand in frustration. "I don't know who is capable of running the pulp mill," he said, "but as of today, it won't be Ryder McGowan."

Aaron finally stopped pacing, ripped off his tie and shook it at the ceiling. "We've requested a tow truck down from Dar," he said. "I figure it will be months before we get the spare parts so it can be repaired. Out of some one hundred and forty vehicles on site, twenty-one are actually running—and some of those barely running."

"Oh, Aaron, you don't need this," Anna said.

Suddenly he stopped, smiled, looked down at Anna with narrowed eyes. "So, we need a backup, and the Suzuki is our backup. Besides," he said, "I hate to see you holed up here, so if you want to drive around the village, the Suzuki is yours to use."

Indeed, the next week Chief Shasani commandeered Jabari and their Land Cruiser to bring him and his contingent from the Ministry to the mill, take them to the coal mine and then drive them back to Dar. The car returned with the brake pads worn and suspension bushings shot. Jabari and Anna took the Suzuki to Iringa to buy flour, sugar, chicken, ground coffee and out-of-date seeds for the vegetable garden. They took Simba to the vet.

"She's always crying for food," Anna said. The vet checked her over and said she was fine. "She's just hungry. You should have named her Africa."

§§§

In the late afternoon, after they returned from Iringa, Jabari took the Suzuki to Aaron at the mill, and Anna left the house to walk through the village. The children stopped their running, jumping, twirling rocks tied to the end of pieces of string. They stood rigid, the younger ones hiding behind their taller brothers or sisters. "*Jambo*," Anna said.

The bigger children smiled broadly, many with teeth missing or misaligned, and the smaller ones slowly peered out from behind their brothers or sisters, then quickly hid again. "*Habari?*" she asked.

They didn't respond. She wondered if they would ever accept her, ever answer her in friendship rather than hide from her in fear.

She continued walking down the hill to the market and bargained for cinnamon sold by the spoonful, then for two tobacco tins of rice. A tall man wearing only a loincloth and carrying a spear kept his distance but trailed her from stall to stall. His hair, discolored with dust, was long, a wild mass of ringlets, and his eyes were bloodshot. She asked the vendors in the market who he was, but they just shook their heads. The peanut vendor said that maybe he was just curious about her; maybe he'd never seen a *mzungu* before.

As Anna headed back up the hill, the man with the spear disappeared into the bush, and she wondered where he could live to have never seen a white person. She thought of her early anxieties: the sound of laughter outside her window that first night; the snake in the garden; Aaron late from his meeting in the city. Now she was stalked by a nearly naked man with a spear, and, while she was startled, she was, surprisingly, not afraid.

That evening after dinner, Aaron trudged down the hall to work at his computer. It wasn't the first time Anna had lost Aaron to his work; not the first time she'd gone off exploring with her camera or retreated to the darkroom to spend long hours doing work of her own. She enjoyed the creative engagement, the pursuit of the endless "what if's" that emerged with every photograph. Sometimes she hardly knew time was passing and was startled to find Aaron home and waiting for her.

But that night she retreated to the bedroom to read. Alan Paton led her down Kumalo's lovely road, across his grass-covered hills and into his valley on its journey to the sea. She could hear him cry for his beloved country, the very foundation shattered by a generation of youth leaving the old villages and traditions, seeking—seeking blindly—a replacement in the cities, the mines, the emerging industries.

Anna set the novel aside, wondering if the workers in Ahadi retained the rituals, the values of their childhood villages; if their children would develop new rituals based on their upbringing in this manufactured town. What would happen to those children when they left school? Primary school was free, but secondary school costly. What future would they find here, or would they drift off to the city?

Anna got up and went to the back bedroom. She lifted Aaron's hand from the desk and brushed her lips across the fine hairs on his knuckles, then led him out the patio door. Like their first night in Ahadi, they held each other under a sky saturated with stars. This night Anna felt sheltered rather than daunted by the vast, the glorious African sky.

A Tanzanian Story

CHAPTER THIRTEEN: BABU BUNGARA

$\mathcal{T}$he rains dwindled, and the temperature rose into the 'eighties. News from the world filtered in slowly and usually a week or so late. Occasionally, copies of the *International Herald-Tribune*, *Time* or *Newsweek* were passed around. In early July Anna read that a June 21 earthquake in Iran had killed 50,000 people. A recent stampede in a pedestrian tunnel in Mecca had killed 1,426 pilgrims. Saudi King Fahd called it God's will.

Absorbed by the *Herald-Tribune*, Anna didn't hear Jabari arrive in a borrowed Land Cruiser to take her to the store at the tea plantation. She looked up to see him, clearly distraught, pacing the driveway in front of the house. She grabbed her purse and told Tobias she hoped to be back by noon. But as they drove toward the gate, Jabari was still distracted, fidgety. Anna asked him to pull over.

"Something's troubling you," she said. "Can you tell me what it is?"

Jabari told Anna that his daughter, Johani, had been sick for a week, every day worse, and he wanted to take her to Babu Bungara. Anna told him to turn around and go back to the house. He should drive the Land Cruiser to the mill and leave the key with the GM. She would meet him there with the Suzuki and they'd pick up Johani and go to Babu.

"But the GM told me to take you to the tea plantation."

Anna wanted to relieve Jabari's fears for his daughter. Also, she wanted to meet this healer, whom Hami and Jabari trusted. She wanted to confirm what she had long felt, that

117

native healers knew of cures that modern medical doctors had never been taught. "The GM will understand," she said. "I will write a note which you can give him with the car keys."

When Jabari came out of the mill, he handed Anna a message from Aaron. "Leave your camera at home—and don't let the Suzuki key out of your sight. I love you, crazy woman."

So she told Jabari she would drive. They stopped by his house, and he carefully laid six-year old Johani across the back seat. She was shivering, and, at the same time, sweat formed at her hairline, dampening the neat braids woven back from her forehead. Her large eyes were partly closed, crusted, and her skin appeared dusty gray.

"Jabari," Anna said, "I didn't know your daughter was so sick. Perhaps we should go to the doctor at the mill or to the hospital in Iringa."

"My wife took her yesterday to the doctor. She waited three hours and then learned he had already left for Dar Es Salaam. If Babu says she should go to the hospital, I will somehow get her there."

Jabari's story upset Anna, and she knew that Aaron would be upset, too.

"We'll hear what Babu has to say. If we need to, we can ask the GM to find you a ride to get her to Iringa."

Jabari nodded. "Thank you, Mama GM. That is a very good plan."

Anna parked the Suzuki at the end of the road just beyond the market. Jabari wrapped Johani in a white sweater and carried her in his arms. She was awake but weak. She gave her father all the smile she seemed to be able to muster and rubbed her eyelids. Anna reached out, touched the child's forehead, silently prayed, "Dear God, tell me we are doing the right thing."

They walked down a dirt path under a canopy of palms. The path narrowed and twisted, first left then right, and the palms gave way to clumps of small, flowering plants sheltered beneath larger shrubs.

The same man she'd seen before was walking toward them, his eyes on the ground. He still wore only a loincloth and carried a spear. He looked up and watched them, then turned and jumped over a shrub, disappearing into the woods beyond.

"Do you know that man?" Anna asked Jabari.

"Yes. I have seen him before. I think he lives in the bush beyond Tobias' house. It's somehow strange. Nobody has ever heard him speak."

§§§

Anna expected Babu Bungara to have ghostly eyes and hennaed hair; to wear animal skins draped with beads and feathers; she expected his hut to be covered in cobwebs, musty and reeking of incense. But when she pulled back the red curtain and they entered the wattle hut, she was relieved to find an immaculate anteroom smelling faintly of mint.

A young man wearing clean blue jeans and a Harvard tee-shirt put a thick textbook down on the table beside him, rose from a rattan chair and greeted them. He told them his name was Samwell. He took Johani from Jabari's arms and gently placed her down on a couch covered with a clean white sheet. As he adjusted the sweater to cover her trembling legs, he invited Jabari and Anna to sit in the folding chairs next to the couch.

Instead, Jabari pulled a handkerchief from his pocket, knelt beside the couch and wiped the perspiration from his daughter's face. As he did so, droplets of sweat began to form on his forehead. He wiped them with the handkerchief and looked up at Anna, his expression a mixture of fear and worry.

"My grandfather has just now finished with a visitor," Samwell said. "I will tell him you are here." He slipped through a white curtain into a back room.

They waited only a few moments before Samwell returned, picked up Johani and led them through the curtain. Jabari's eyes never wavered from his daughter. His stance was tense, as if ready to pounce, to grab his child if anything went amiss.

Samwell lowered Johani onto a bare cot in front of Babu Bungara who sat cross-legged on a slightly-raised platform. Above him a pair of matching glass kerosene lanterns hung from the ceiling to illuminate the room. On every wall, reaching to the ceiling, were rows of red-painted shelves. On the shelves were glass bottles in a variety of shapes and sizes. They appeared to be filled with herbs, spices, seeds, liquids; with small, preserved bugs, beads and an assortment of white, pink and blue pills.

Babu Bungara's eyes sparkled, and his mouth turned up in a gentle smile. His short, curly hair and trimmed mustache were pure white. He wore a white button-down short-sleeved shirt, open at the collar to reveal a thatch of white chest hair. A stethoscope dangled from his neck. He looked like a doctor in a pharmaceutical ad, exuding confidence, and Anna began to wonder if he might not actually be able to heal Johani.

On the shelf behind him was a blood-pressure machine, mortar and pestle, a stack of white Styrofoam coffee cups wrapped in plastic, an otoscope for examining the ears, a thin, silver flashlight, pair of tongs, small brass bell and several closed blue instrument boxes. Steam rose from a silver chafing dish braced over a can of Sterno. Anna looked for the source of the water for the steam, but there was no sink in the room.

Babu Bungara acknowledged them, stepped down from the platform and immediately bent over Johani, who squirmed and cried. Jabari reached out for his daughter, but Bungara shook his head. Jabari stepped back. Bungara slowly passed his hand over Johani's face. Only then her mouth relaxed. She eyed him with wonder and became peacefully still.

He felt both sides of her neck, carefully lifted the sheet and felt the lymph nodes under her armpits. Then he put the stethoscope to his ears and listened to her heart and lungs. He opened one of the boxes behind him, pulled out a white tissue and dipped it in the steaming water before dabbing the edges of her eyes. Again, she squirmed, began to cry. Again, Jabari rose. Once more, Bungara calmed Johani by passing his hand over her face.

After looking closely at the residue on the tissue, Bungara tossed it in a wastebasket beside the platform and bent over Johani. As he began to pull Johani's skirt up, Anna involuntarily reached out to stop him, but Bungara looked at Anna solemnly and shook his finger at her. She backed off. He rolled Johani's underpants down part way then gently rolled her on her side. He pressed her skin, her hands, her toes, redressed her, then took the flashlight from the shelf. He asked her to open her mouth, turned on the flashlight and peered inside.

He asked her a question. She nodded, "*Nndio*." He asked another. "*Hapa*," she whispered and pointed to her lower left jaw. Jabari, still watchful, still tense, translated for Anna. "He wants to know where it hurts."

With the alacrity of a much younger man, Bungara went to a shelf across the room, removed a jar of large seeds, extracted three, ground them in the pestle, poured them into a Styrofoam cup from the stack then added steaming water. He turned his back to Anna and Jabari, shook the cup and muttered an incantation in some strange-sounding tongue that Anna was certain was not Swahili nor any other language she had ever heard.

Anna gave Jabari a questioning look. She was surprised, undeniably concerned, that this man, who seemed so professional, so thorough, considering the limitations of an office with no water or electricity, was reverting to age-old customs, practices she understood to be native healing—juju, witchcraft. But Jabari now appeared to be more relaxed. He whispered, "It's okay, Mama."

Babu Bungara faced them again and raised Johani's head. "*Kunywa hii,*" he said. Johani took a tentative sip of the potion, then another. "*Nzuri,*" he said, then "*Tena.* Again."

Johani pressed her lips tightly together and shook her head. Jabari took the cup from Bungara, sat on the cot and held it to her lips. "*Tena,*" he repeated softly. She closed her eyes and swallowed the rest of the potion. "*Nzuri,* Johani," he said, then handed the cup back to Bungara and took his child in his arms.

Bungara pondered a row of glass jars on the far shelf and finally pulled out a small string of yellow beads. Again, he muttered something in a mysterious language before tying the strand around Johani's left ankle.

Then the doctor spoke to Jabari and Anna in English, saying that the potion would soothe the sore in Johani's mouth, reduce her fever and keep her from feeling more pain. "The amulet, the beads," he said, "are very powerful, and will fight the evil spirits hovering around her."

Anna shook her head. Amulets. Beads. Evil spirits. She was ready to bolt for the hospital when Bungara said, "I have examined her thoroughly and done what I can, but don't have the medicine to cure her. It may be a form of tuberculosis. The doctors at the hospital in Iringa can tell you what you need to know."

"Thank you," Anna said, "We will go there now."

Jabari sniffed back evident sadness and smiled at Johani. He held his daughter close to him and looked to the doctor for reassurance.

But Babu Bungara just turned and stepped up onto the platform. He sat and crossed his legs then reached behind him and rang the brass bell—once, twice, three times— before raising his eyes. He appeared to be withdrawing into a trance.

Anna watched him carefully. Except for the lack of a feather emerging from a headband, he seemed to her to now resemble the Barnetts' sculpted shaman. His expression, facing them, was clearly one of deep contemplation. Anna stepped to the side to search his profile for signs of sorrow or hope but found neither.

His grandson, Samwell, led them back to the anteroom. Jabari adjusted the sweater across Johani's shoulders and conferred with the young man. He shifted Johani to his left arm to reach for his wallet.

"How much?" Anna asked.

"2,000 *shillingis*," Jabari said.

Anna dug into her purse and handed Samwell two thousand-shilling notes. He wrote a receipt, and they returned down the path to the car. Jabari held his daughter to his chest and sniffed back his tears.

§§§

When they arrived at the house at one o'clock, Aaron had finished lunch and was sitting on the patio, reading a document and drinking a cup of coffee. Within minutes, after Anna had related the story of their visit to Babu Bungara, they were all piling into the Land Cruiser to take Johani to Iringa.

The doctors there first said that Johani had tonsillitis, but they wanted to keep the child in the hospital for a few days to observe her. Jabari would stay with her. Anna was to notify Jabari's wife, Dafina, to come to Iringa to oversee their daughter's care. Dafina's niece, living just outside the village, could move into the house in Ahadi to look after the twin boys.

Three days later, when Jabari returned to Ahadi, he said that the doctors had changed the diagnosis to a form of latent, non-infectious tuberculosis, but where it had settled, or how, or when it will emerge as infectious, they were not sure. Johani would remain in the hospital.

There was no kitchen in the hospital, so family members of the patients went to the vendors in the courtyard to buy what they could for food. When Anna and Aaron returned to Iringa, they took chicken soup, chicken with rice, fruit salad, peanut butter cookies, soft drinks and boiled water for Johani and her mother. They searched the markets for toys to engage a bed-ridden six-year old. Anna found only a soft cloth doll with bright blue eyes and purple yarn for hair. She took it to Johani who laughed and held the doll close, then unbuttoned and buttoned the overall straps before falling asleep. Anna tucked the doll under the covers next to the child and smoothed Johani's hair.

As she left the room, Anna turned to look once more at

124

the sleeping child. "Have mercy," she prayed, silently but fervently. "Please, if there is such a thing as mercy, this child deserves to live."

In two weeks, Johani was released from the hospital, but she was back again after two days. The doctor seemed unable to say why her fever had returned or why she continued to break out in rashes. Anna suggested she should be tested for an immune deficiency. The doctor just shook his head.

"It's not likely," he said. "Usually, the parents don't survive, but the children—"

He turned to leave the room, then stopped at the door and looked back at Johani. "So many orphans," he whispered.

A Tanzanian Story

CHAPTER FOURTEEN: THE KARANGAMAN

*A*s the dry season progressed, water was limited to the village except for the houses at the top of the hill. Aaron confronted the town manager, and water became available throughout the village from seven to nine in the morning and from five to seven at night.

But Priscilla Fuller demanded water all day long. "My house boy can't clean up after breakfast and wash the clothes if the water is cut off at nine. And how is the gardener expected to water all the flowers and the grass? She doesn't come to work until 8:30." Priscilla threatened to go back to Arkansas. Anna told her that was always an option.

Hami and Anna finished regrouping the roses and the daisies to require less water. In Iringa, Anna found a nozzle that rotated to turn the hose off while it was being carried from plant to plant. She bought three and gave one to Becky Barnett and one to Priscilla Fuller. "It will just take longer to water the garden," Priscilla said and handed it back. Anna wondered if she could give it to someone else, but, to her knowledge, none of her African neighbors had an outdoor faucet, much less a hose.

Each afternoon, the sun dried up the new garden pond. Anna and Hami filled it with dirt. On a trip to the market in Mbeya, Anna was surprised to discover an artist displaying a four-foot tall bronze statue of a malachite sunbird, his long, thin tail trailing behind him like a blade of lemon grass, his head high, eyes focused whimsically at the sky. She bought

127

it and placed it in the thinking garden.

At night, the stars were brighter than ever, and the sunbird appeared to shimmer in the dark.

§§§

Hami came to work earlier each day to water the garden. Anna watched him tug at the hose which had caught on a clump of white calla lilies. He twisted the new nozzle. The water went off, and Anna smiled. Hami untangled the hose and darted back to the vegetable *shamba* to aim the water at a row of Brussels sprouts. The sprouts were nearly as tall as Hami and ready to harvest.

In the peanut patch at the front end of the vegetable garden, raw peanuts were put in the week before, and green plants were already emerging. Anna asked Hami to add more manure since the last crop was small. Hami said he thought someone was stealing them. Anna suspected that he was right.

"Just make sure they're worth stealing," she said.

"But, Mama," he said, "I have worked hard to make them grow."

"Let's just see what happens," she said.

Hami twisted the nozzle off and ran to the shed. As Anna left the *shamba*, he was pushing the wheelbarrow toward the manure pile and shaking his head.

That morning, Anna felt particularly isolated in her house at the top of the hill. She took a basket from the pantry and left to walk the two kilometers down to the market, though she needed nothing for sale there.

The first stalls were filled with rows of miniature boxes of Omo soap powder and jars of Kimbo shortening, a scattering of Dabega chili sauce.

"*Jambo*," the market women said. Anna smiled.

"*Jambo. Jambo*," she said and walked on, swinging her basket past the rough plywood tables. She paused to look at small pyramids of tomatoes and onions surrounded by mounds of tiny, blackened silver fish.

"*Jambo,*" the women said and pointed to their stacks of tomatoes and onions.

"*Jambo*," Anna said and hurried past the strong odor of fish.

She stopped at the stall of the karangaman—the peanut seller. He had a long face, kolanut brown, which dimmed to black under his eyes, around his mouth and chin. He was tall, sinewy, powerful like a python. Taut muscles stretched across his shoulders and coiled down his arms. She imagined that, like generations of his ancestors, he'd carried sacks of peanuts on his head from the time he was a child. And she imagined his wife, like her ancestors, carrying on her head sacks of maize, pots of water, stacks of firewood and, on her back, a fourth or fifth child who would grow up to plant *karanga* and pray for good rains.

The karangaman moved a beer bottle cap across a hand-painted checkers board, then turned around. His mouth softened into a slow grin. His teeth were small, even, surprisingly white. He greeted her: "*Jambo*, Mama GM."

Anna was startled that he knew who she was, but, of course, everyone in Ahadi, whether she'd met them or not, knew who she was. She felt a brief sense of pride, realizing all the while that the only reason she was recognized was because she was married to Aaron. But she was proud of Aaron, proud to be his wife.

Of course, she was aware of the growing equal rights movement. In high school, she had spent time in the barely-integrated South and deplored the tensions which persisted.

One of her good friends entered the University of Georgia at the same time as Charlayne Hunter-Gault and refused to take gym classes with a black woman. Anna never spoke to her friend again.

She knew that, as a woman, she'd been underpaid out of college compared to men with similar jobs. She knew it was wrong to deny women the same opportunities as men. She still blamed herself for distrusting Carina Sorenstam, an evidently capable woman deserving of a better job at Transnational.

Had she stayed in Vermont to pursue her profession, would she have been happier? No. The choice she had made was the right choice—to be here with Aaron and to support him as she could. But she also knew she needed to sustain her self-respect, and she could only do so on her own, independently of Aaron. His position was proscribed. If the company had provided her with a job description, she assumed it was to run the household so that Aaron could do his job. With little effort on her part, the household was running smoothly. It was time she had a new job description.

§§§

The karangaman watched Anna closely as she ran her hand through a pile of large, smooth peanuts. While eating anything uncooked was risky, and the unroasted nut would be soft and bitter, she pulled a pink-skinned peanut from the middle of the pile and popped it in her mouth. He seemed to enjoy her boldness and laughed.

"How much?" she asked.

"Fifty *shillingis.*"

"Oh, so expensive. *Sana ghali*. Forty," she said.

He appeared to consider, then wagged his head slowly like a gecko pondering his prey.

"No, Mama. Fifty," he said.

She turned toward the next stall. "Forty-five," he called after her.

"Okay." The deal was settled.

The dickering over price was not, to Anna, a contest about money though she suspected that, to the karangaman, every shilling was precious. He was asking her to pay ten cents for a tobacco tin of peanuts which would have cost her ten times more in America.

She bargained with the karangaman because she wanted to respect him, and she wanted him to respect her, which meant he would offer, and she would accept a fair price. Yet, to Anna, the transaction felt more like a treaty between two disparate nations, each pretending to be kindred to the other, each knowing better.

She wanted to give him more; she wanted to sweep through the market handing out shillings to all the women sweating behind their stalls; candy and toys to all the runny-nosed, big-bellied children; shoes and books to everyone. She wanted to believe that she could cure Africa of poverty, illiteracy, sickness, though she knew she was dreaming. All the shillings she had, all the gifts she could give wouldn't save one of them. She thought of the gifts she'd bought for Jabari's daughter. A coloring book. A doll. Would either of them make Johani well?

The karangaman filled a dented can with peanuts, and she grabbed a handful more to dribble over the top of the can until it overflowed. The karangaman laughed and dumped the peanuts into her basket. They played the game ten times.

"Four hundred fifty *shillinigis*," the karangaman said.

"What, no *kidogo*?" she asked. He laughed again and plowed through the pile with his tin can, loaded it until it overflowed, then tossed the peanuts in her basket. She handed him five hundred-shilling notes. He reached under the soiled burlap which served as a tablecloth and pulled out a greasy, torn fifty-shilling bill, more gray than its original pink. She waved it away.

"*Kidogo*," she said. "*Asante Sana*."

He grinned and turned back to his checkers board.

As Anna started up the hill toward home, she wondered how many of the peanuts she had just bought grew in her own garden.

CHAPTER FIFTEEN: ALLAH, MY CHILD

*T*hey had been in Ahadi nearly six months. In that time, they'd made four trips to Dar, and now they were on the road again. Jabari asked if they could make a quick stop at the hospital in Iringa where they found his daughter, Johani, asleep in her bed in the children's ward. Tucked in beside her was the cloth doll with the bright blue eyes and hair of purple yarn, and a pink crayon lay next to her hand. Beside it was the coloring book, open to the picture of the zebra. The white stripes were filled in, pink alternating with green.

Aaron and Anna slipped out to give Jabari and his daughter some privacy, and when Jabari met them at the car, he was holding the picture of the zebra. He opened the car door to show them the page and smiled wistfully. "This is somehow beautiful, don't you think?"

"All zebras should be so magnificent," Anna said.

Jabari went around to the boot and pulled out his worn black duffel bag. He slipped the picture in between the folds of his roaring lion tee-shirt.

All the way to Dar, Anna felt the weight of that pink and green zebra in Jabari's bag. It was a heavy weight, indeed.

§§§

As Aaron attended meetings at the ministry, Jabari took Anna to the shops to replenish the goods they needed. They returned to the sagging building which housed the photo studio. Again, the heavy-set Indian proprietor was asleep in a chair. He woke up and said they could buy everything in the shop, since he was going out of business.

A Tanzanian Story

"Oh, I'm sorry," Anna said. "What will you do?"

He shrugged his shoulders. "Don't worry, lady. I have a rich uncle." He laughed, his mouth wide open, gums bright pink.

His shelves were even more sparse than before, but he had what Anna needed: twenty packets of Kodak developer, two years out of date; fifteen packets of fixer, only a year out of date. Each would make a gallon of chemicals. Anna asked him if he had any stop bath on hand. He pointed to two jugs on the lower shelf. Each would make twenty gallons. She took both.

There were only two dusty packets of 8x10 Kodak photographic paper, one matte, one gloss. Anna figured if she cut them into smaller sizes she'd have enough to last a while. Four boxes of Ilford 400-speed black and white film were left on the shelf. She added them to the pile.

"You don't want anything else?" he asked. He took her into the back room and showed her his Beseler enlarger, a full-size, professional model, similar to the one she had in Vermont. It was tempting, but the compact unit worked just fine, and she'd only be frustrated trying to make gallery-quality prints in her small Ahadi bathroom.

§§§

The next day was Aaron's birthday, and Anna wanted to buy him something special and take him out for a nice dinner. When he arrived back at the Oyster Bay hotel late in the afternoon, they walked over to the nearby carver's row. Aaron appeared to be struck by a 4-foot tall, solid ebony statue of an old man with his dog. The man, shoulders stooped, forehead wrinkled, expression determined, was bare-chested with a *kanga* wrapped around his waist. He held his dog's leash tight in his right hand while the dog playfully leapt at the water gourd roped through the fingers of his left hand.

Anna asked Aaron if she could buy it for him. "Yes," he said, "I'd like that. But you have to get it at the right price."

"I'll let you bargain for it," Anna said. Aaron became so adamant at refusing the carver's price, Anna was afraid they wouldn't own this treasure. She began to wonder whether Aaron liked it as much as she did. But he finally agreed upon a price and asked her if she had twenty-five thousand shillings. She reached into the zippered compartment of her purse, pulled out the wad of notes left over from the morning shopping and handed it to Aaron. He counted the money, shook his head and added six thousand shillings from his wallet.

"Happy birthday," she said. "I'll cash in a traveler's check and pay you back."

"No," he said. "You paid for the man. I just paid for the dog. Actually, the dog is my gift for Murray."

Aaron bent down to eye the smiling dog more closely. "Do you think Murray will like her?" He hefted the 40-pound carving onto his shoulder. When the porter saw them approaching the hotel, he raced to take the statue from Aaron. The porter lifted it, upright, atop his head and started up the stairs.

On the way back to Ahadi, they stopped overnight at Mikumi. Jabari wore his lion shirt and seemed right at home. They got out of the car to watch a herd of zebras in the distance. Anna kept seeing them as Johani had colored them, pink and green. She couldn't bring herself to take a photograph and handed her camera to Jabari. Instead of focusing on the zebras, he turned around and took a picture of the two of them, just shy of a kiss. Aaron saw the camera, stepped back and laughed. Then he nodded at Jabari, pulled

Anna close to him and finished the kiss.

§§§

They turned off the highway to go to Iringa, and while Aaron
and Anna shopped for meat and cheese, Jabari went to the
hospital. It was early afternoon when Aaron pulled up beside
the front breezeway, crowded with waiting patients, among
them a woman with a carved wooden leg; a man with a large
bandage over his right eye; a listless child lolling in his
mother's *kanga*.

Then Anna spotted Jabari sitting on the curb, his head
in his hands, his shoulders quaking. A small paper sack lay
beside him with purple yarn—the hair of Johani's doll—
poking out of the top.

"Oh, no," Anna said. God had ignored her prayer, and
her worst fears for the child had been realized. Aaron looked
out the window, shut down the engine, threw the keys on the
dashboard and leapt from the car.

He put a hand on Jabari's shoulder. Anna grabbed the keys,
jumped down from the passenger seat and ran to Jabari. He
finally looked up, first at Aaron then at Anna. "I was here just
two days ago," he said. "How can this be? Oh, my sweet girl.
My child. Johani." His face was streaked with tears. He wept
openly and, again, covered his face with his hands.

Aaron knelt beside him. Between low moans, Jabari
spoke a few words, his voice raspy: "Maybe pneumonia…
infection…TB. The nurse, she said maybe…maybe AIDS.
My child. All alone. Allah, my child."

Anna sat on the curb beside Jabari. All three of them were
crying. Anna shuddered for the loss of this innocent child.
And she shuddered again, thinking about what the nurse had
said. HIV was raging through Africa, pursuing truckers and
company drivers, their families across the Trans-African

Highway. Yet the killer's origins, its source, its detection remained a mystery to most of them—an evil spirit with no name. Maybe Johanna had died from one of the other dozen insidious killers roaming this land. Or maybe the nurse was right and the doctor wrong.

§§§

Jabari didn't want to leave the hospital, the place where Johani lay in a small refrigerated box, never again to open her eyes. He said he would remain on a bench on the veranda until his wife arrived. When not at the hospital, she was staying at a cousin's flat in Iringa and would surely come before nightfall. Together, they would take Johani to his mother's village, fifty kilometers north.

"Johani will become an ancestor in the village," Jabari said. He sniffed back tears. "An ancestor at six years old."

"You and your wife need each other now," Anna said. "Let us take you to her." He finally agreed.

"I'll drive," Aaron said. "You show me the way."

Jabari held the sack close to his chest and got into the back seat. Halfway down the main street, crowded with shops and market stalls, he told Aaron to turn right and follow the road. After a few more turns he told them to stop at a small apartment complex. The two-story buildings were white, streaked with stains and dappled with mold.

"Do you have transportation?" Aaron asked.

"No sir," Jabari said. "My wife's cousin is a widow with two small children."

"I can send a truck from Ahadi," Aaron said.

"Thank you, sir, we will be okay. The carpenter who stays near the hospital—" Jabari hesitated, then continued, his voice rough, a whisper. "The carpenter is already at work on the box. He has—he said he knows of a truck."

"Can't we help in any way?" Anna asked.

"Mama, please tell my wife's niece who takes care of the twins that Dafina and I—" His voice broke, and he started over. "Dafina, Johani and I have gone to my mother's village and will return within a week. I don't want the boys to know until we can tell them ourselves."

"Of course," she said. "Is there nothing more?"

Jabari shook his head and reached over the back seat to pull out his duffle bag. He got out of the car. Anna rolled down the window, reached out to touch his hand, which was still holding tight to the sack with Johani's belongings. "Do you want us to wait to make sure they are here?" she asked.

He looked up at the building. "I see my wife sitting by the window. Thank you, Mama. It's okay."

Aaron handed Anna a wad of shilling notes which she gave to Jabari. He took them, thanked Aaron and straightened his shirt. They waited while he walked slowly toward the building, head down, carrying his duffle over his shoulder and clenching the sack to his chest as if he were still holding onto his child.

When Jabari had entered the building and had time to climb the stairs, Aaron started the car, then turned it off again. "I can't imagine what he's going through." He wiped his hand across his eyes and sat for several minutes, his head against the steering wheel. Anna remained focused on the second-story window. Finally, the figure in the chair rose and disappeared into the room. A few moments later, Aaron turned the key in the ignition, and they drove back through Iringa to the gravel road toward Ahadi.

The air became chilly as they ascended the escarpment. Anna leaned her head against Aaron's shoulder. They didn't speak the whole way home.

CHAPTER SIXTEEN: A LONG-AGO MOTHER

*I*t was twilight when they arrived at the house. Jonas Shao, the finance manager, was waiting outside the door—a short man wearing a white polo shirt and a green sport jacket.

As soon as they stepped wearily from the car, Shao approached Aaron. "Good evening, Mr. Chadwick," he said, his face breaking into a massive smile. Aaron didn't smile in return.

"God has sent me here to speak to you on a business of some urgency," he said.

"Nothing can be as urgent," Aaron said, "as my wife and I unloading this car and pouring ourselves a cold drink."

Aaron opened the boot and reached for the box of groceries they'd bought in Iringa. Shao rushed to the back of the car and leaned in toward Aaron. "But Mr. Chadwick, this is a matter of great concern."

"We will talk at the mill first thing in the morning," Aaron said.

Shao didn't move. "In the morning, Mr. Shao. I will see you in my office at seven."

Aaron lifted the box, and Shao was forced to duck. "*Kwaheri,*" Aaron said. "Sleep well."

Aaron carried the box to the doorstep. Anna turned the key in the lock, grabbed Simba waiting at the door, and they went inside. When they stepped back outside to get more packages, Jonas Shao was sitting on the front step.

"Okay. Tell me in ten words what this is about," Aaron said.

"It is about a matter of the very most extreme importance," Shao said.

"That's eleven words," Aaron said. "I think the matter can wait until morning. I'll see you then."

"But—" Shao said. Just then Simba dashed out, and Shao jumped up, backed away, turned and hurried to his car.

By the time Aaron had retrieved the carving of the man and his dog from the car, Jonas Shao was gone. Aaron carried the statue inside and placed it next to the bookcase, so it faced the front door. Simba followed Aaron inside and peered intently at the figure. She moved closer and nonchalantly rubbed up against the dog.

While Anna put away the perishables, Aaron poured himself a scotch, then a glass of wine for her. "Aaron, aren't you worried that something serious —"

Aaron laughed. "Mr. Shao often has matters of great importance to discuss, usually having to do with his or his staff's compensation, or with procuring a bid for a crony. Whatever it is, it can wait until morning."

He took a swallow of his drink. "But, something serious *has* happened," he said. "It happened today at the hospital in Iringa."

"Yes," Anna said. "I can think of nothing else." Aaron's eyes held hers for a long time, then he finally looked away.

"Let's go outside," he said.

They each grabbed a light jacket and stepped onto the patio. The stars were just emerging, stars which Johani would never learn to name. That night, not even the stars offered Anna solace or inspiration; they were just there— far away, cold and indifferent, bearing no relationship to earth, to Africa, to God, life, death, Jabari, Johani.

Anna shivered and turned from Aaron. He drew her to

him and held her from behind, held her as if to keep her upright and warm.

But she was still shivering, and, as much as she didn't want to leave his embrace, she told Aaron she was going inside. He swallowed the last of his drink and followed her through the door. Then he turned to take one last look at the sky. "Despite all the suffering, it's a magnificent country." He bowed his head. "*Mungu ibariki Africa.*"

Anna knew *Mungu* was the word for God but asked him what *ibariki* meant. "Bless," he said. "God bless Africa. It's from the national anthem. There's also a line: *Tubariki watoto wa Africa.* Bless us, children of Africa, and I think that means all of us, our beginnings created a long, long time ago under these same stars."

Anna had often walked through this garden and intuitively felt, deep beneath the soil, the remnants of roughly-built homes, fragments from a clay pot, a stone spoon, ochre bones of a nearly-erect woman—long-ago mother to the long-ago mother of Jabari Tamin, Babu Bungara, Catherine Dennison, Glenna Sikes; long ago mother to Aaron's mother—and to her own.

She thought about all that had changed and not changed since those long-ago times. "Bless us," she said. "Bless us, save us all, children of Africa, the living and—."

She could no longer hold back her tears.

A Tanzanian Story

CHAPTER SEVENTEEN:
THE BASEBALL GAME

Christopher sent a box with band-aids, antibiotic cream and Ziploc bags. He included the latest edition of *Newsweek*. Saddam Hussein was on the cover, and the headline read "Baghdad's Bully." President George Bush had launched Operation Desert Storm.

"Life in Vermont is pretty dull, mostly due to so much rain," he wrote. "But I actually got to help produce a story about a freight train derailment in Sharon—the biggest story of the summer—except that Bernie Sanders is running for congress. I hope I'll get to cover a rally next week."

Christopher added that his boyhood friend, Tom Andrews, had joined the Marines. Anna paused, concerned, hoping her son would stay on the path he'd chosen. She believed he was learning a lot at WVTA, and after graduate school he'd be able to move into a job that would send him on the adventures he craved.

She reread his letter three times and was on her way to the kitchen when she heard voices at the front door. "*Hodi! Hodi!*"

Becky Barnett had arrived with Grace Kapera, the head mistress of the primary school: a slender, elegant, serene and highly intelligent woman, so aptly named Grace. They took cups of tea to the patio and planned together how to create a library for the school. Aaron would ask the mill carpenter to build bookcases. They would reach out to friends in America

143

for donations of books and games to fill the shelves.

Anna was elated. She felt, at last, a connection, though quite thin, to the village of Ahadi. She had been assigned a small job with a clear-cut description.

That afternoon, the boiler at the mill was fully repaired, and the steam turbine, out of commission for two years, was finally back in operation, so power company cutbacks could take less of a toll on production. Smoke rose from the towers at the paper mill. Aaron arrived home a happier man.

§§§

The next week Grace Kapera called on Anna again, asking if she might fill in for a week while the Grade 7 English teacher travelled home to her village for her father's funeral. Anna readily agreed.

The first day was tough. Anna tried gentle cajoling, joking, even some mild ribbing to get the students to raise their heads off their desks and participate in the lesson on personal pronouns. Finally, she told them they would play a game.

She wrote the alphabet across the top of the blackboard and drew a hangman scaffold beneath it. Then she wrote: "Mama GM was _ _ _ _ _ _." She told the students to select a letter to begin. The girl in the left-hand seat in the back row—Busara, the smallest and shyest of the girls—would select first.

"A," Busara whispered.

"Excellent," Anna said. "There is an 'A'". She filled in the first letter. "Mama GM was A_ _ _ _ _."

Anna pointed to a tall boy in the third row.

"B!" he said.

"No, no 'B'," Anna said and drew a circle for the head. Then she explained that every wrong answer would add to

144

the figure. If the man she was drawing had a head, body, two arms and two legs, he would be hung. Their job was to keep him from hanging. "Think about the letters most used in English. Start with those."

The drawing had a head, a body and an arm before the next student said "E."

"Good," Anna said. "Mama GM was A_ _ EE_."

She was afraid the game would be lost, and the lesson also lost. So she gave a hint to Gladness, the next student, who appeared to be the oldest of the group, the most developed and apparently quite popular among her classmates. "What letter makes 'giraffe' more than one giraffe?"

Gladness just shook her head.

"One giraffe, two –"

Gladness rolled her eyes. "Giraffes," she said.

"So the letter is?"

The boy next to her raised his hand.

"Yes, Jeffari."

"S!" he exclaimed.

Anna filled in the letter. "Absolutely! AS_EE_."

Now all the class was sitting up, looking at the board. From the back of the room, little Busara raised her hand. Anna nodded to her.

"L?" she asked, her voice a little louder than before.

"Yes!" Anna filled in the letter. ASLEE_. She yawned widely. "Who knows the answer?"

Half of the children shouted in unison: "Asleep!"

"You got it! Good work. And you kept the man from being hung."

The children laughed.

When Anna walked into the classroom after lunch, Gladness and Jeffari were at the blackboard playing hangman.

Anna smiled. She had won a small victory.

While the students may not have learned all she hoped they would, by the end of the week, not one head remained on a desk. In fact, at the end of the final day, all hands were in the air, begging to be called on to answer a question.

And it was not an easy question: "Tell me in English: "*Upendo ni nini?*—What is love?"

To Anna, the answers were astounding:

"Being happy."

"Making someone happy."

"Believing in something like God."

"Not caring just about yourself."

Gladness jumped up and down to be recognized and said: "Feeling Sexy."

Everyone laughed, some uncomfortably.

Then shy Busara, from the back of the room, not only waved her hand but stood up, begging to be called upon. "Yes," Anna said. "What do you think is love?"

"You can love someone," she said, her voice muffled as she looked down at the floor, "when you try very hard to know them."

"Go on," Anna said.

Busara shuffled her feet. "That's all I know to say." She quickly sat down.

"Yes!" Anna said. "First you learn who they are—and why—then you can understand them. Only then can you begin to love them."

§§§

When the week ended, Anna and Grace Kapera began to work out plans for a voluntary once-a-week after-school enrichment program to start in January, the beginning of the next term.

Anna would teach photography. The choirmaster from the Methodist church would form a chorus. Aaron would give paid time off to mill workers who would teach art, woodworking, business, engineering. Hami's uncle, Mahib Kamala, would teach horticulture. Three mill superintendents had volunteered to coach football, tennis, track. Tobias would hold cooking classes. The children would be rewarded for their talents; they would discover that learning can be fun. The workers would have their first experience at volunteering. Members of the community would be engaged with the primary school as never before. It was Grace Kapera's splendid idea, yet she was generously giving Anna full credit for developing the plan.

§§§

The next time Anna passed through the village with her shopping basket, her camera strapped around her neck, the children, as always, stopped their running, jumping, twirling; stopped bouncing or tossing their new little soccer balls to gape at her. As she looked at them from a distance, she wished Johani were there as well.

She wondered how Jabari and Dafina and their twin boys must feel, seeing other little girls walking to or from school or sitting on their door stoops laughing with a friend.

"*Jambo*," she finally said, and raised the camera to her eye. Unlike the adults, they didn't say "*jambo*" in return, but today, for the first time, they smiled openly, and rather than crouching behind their bigger siblings, the little ones jockeyed for a position in a picture. Anna moved around for several shots from several angles, then beckoned to the smallest girl, but she didn't move. Then Anna took one of the two last balls from her basket and held it out to her. Two bigger boys rushed forward, but she shook her head.

147

"*Hapana.* No," she said, and pointed again to the little girl. The boys laughed, and the little girl came slowly, shyly forward. Anna handed her the ball, and she whispered "*Asante sana*, Mama." Then she grinned at Anna and held the ball in both hands.

Anna pointed to the camera. "Can I take your picture?" she asked. The little girl nodded enthusiastically. Anna took a photograph of her with the ball, then held the camera up to the child's eye and pointed it toward the boys. When Anna clicked it, the little girl flinched and dropped the ball. The boys ran toward her, but the child quickly squatted and grabbed it before the boys could claim it. Anna laughed and gave the little girl a thumbs up. The child responded, her thumb as high as she could reach.

Anna put down her basket and drop kicked the last ball a long way into the vacant lot at the end of the street. The children looked at her in surprise, then turned to race after it. Only the two bigger boys reappeared, throwing the ball back and forth between them, dancing happily after each toss.

She wondered how many balls it would take to provide one for each child in the village.

§§§

Near the school, she heard the distinctive sound of a bat striking a softball, and when she got closer, saw Becky Barnett cheering on a group of girls who looked to be between twelve and fourteen years old. Becky's eyes darted from player to player, all wearing blue skirts and thin white shirts, many of them imprinted with the words "Ahadi Primary School."

The pitcher threw a high lob, but the batter reached over her head and whacked it down the third base line. She reached the burlap bag which served as first base and broke into a

148

kwasa-kwasa, her hips moving back and forth like Kanda Bongo Man. The girls all shrieked, clapped, joined in the dance, and the headmistress, Grace Kapera, smiled her wise smile. "I like this baseball," she said to Anna.

When the next batter, the older girl, Gladness, came up to the plate, Becky put her arms around her, placed her hands over her fingers on the bat and showed her how to swing. The lesson was a success. The pitch was only slightly inside, and Gladness smacked the ball. It soared over second base. There was no outfielder.

"Go!" Becky told her and pointed toward first base. "*Mbio!*" her teammates yelled, telling her to run. Then, to the smaller girl, the runner who hadn't moved off first, Becky yelled "Go!" and pointed her toward second base. The runner lifted her skirt to her thighs and took off. At second base, she stopped again. "*Mbio!*" Grace Kapera called to her. Again, the girl lifted her skirts and ran to third.

Gladness rounded first, then began to run across the infield toward third. "*Hapana!* No!" Becky shouted. She ran with her to second, then pointed her toward third. "*Mbio!*" Becky yelled. "*Mbio!*" her teammates yelled. Gladness laughed and dashed off to third then swung her hips, grabbed the hand of the first runner, and they danced in tandem toward home plate.

Becky sprinted to the outfield, picked up the ball and tossed it to the pitcher who was so engrossed in the excitement that she didn't see it roll past her.

Anna took photographs, then stepped aside to watch the children, joyous with excitement. She took more photographs: groups of players; individual girls; Grace, her head, as always, high, her smile knowing; and Becky, laughing so hard her shoulders were shaking.

Anna was elated by these moments of pure, artless fun for the children of Ahadi. Maybe Becky had the right idea—teaching the children a game which only required a single ball.

§§§

Anna was printing photographs of the baseball game when Eva knocked on the bathroom door. Anna asked her to wait just a moment since she was in the process of developing a picture. When Eva came in, she said that she had finished her work for the day. She looked up at strips of negatives which hung from clothespins on a length of string attached to the shower curtain rod. Then she looked down at the picture of Grace Kapera that Anna had just pulled from the fixer and was holding over the sink. "Oh, my head teacher," Eva said. She came forward to look more closely at the picture. "Mama, how does this happen?"

Anna asked her if she wanted to help, and Eva nodded earnestly. Anna closed the bathroom door, turned on the safelight and put a negative of a picture of Hami in the little Beseler enlarger.

She told Eva to turn the knob until the picture looked right to her. Eva brought the negative image of Hami into focus and began to laugh. "Mama, he is *mzungu!*" she said.

"But that is only temporary," Anna said.

She slid a 4x5 sheet of photo paper through the clamps, set the timer to 45 seconds and told Eva to push the button on the enlarger, then push it again as soon as she heard the timer ring. "Okay, Mama, I am ready," Eva said, her finger poised above the button. "Now!" Anna said. The light went on, and Anna waved a dodger disk over the background to keep it from becoming too dark. The timer went off, and Eva released the button. *"Nzuri,"* Anna said. Eva looked at the paper. "Mama, nothing happen."

"Wait," Anna said. She picked up the paper with the tongs, slid it into the developer, then the stop bath. "Now look," she said.

"Mama, it's magic!" Eva's face was lit with the wonder of the picture appearing.

As Anna slid the print into the fixer, Eva asked if she could keep it. Anna told her she could, but they must make one for Hami as well. When they repeated the process, Anna explained what was happening. "Now you need to make one for me," Anna said.

Eva carefully followed all the steps though she dodged Hami's hair instead of the background, and it came out more gray than black. Still, Anna told her it was good, and asked her if she wanted to help make pictures again.

"Yes, Mama, please!"

The next morning, Anna was heading for the back bedroom when she saw Eva at the ironing board set up in the first bedroom. Propped up against her spray bottle was the picture they printed of Hami. Eva was looking at the picture instead of looking at the jockey shorts she was ironing.

Then Anna noticed Hami weeding the garden in front of the bedroom. He was looking through the window at Eva instead of looking at the weeds.

A Tanzanian Story

CHAPTER EIGHTEEN: THIEFMAN

*T*he three months of small rains began in October. Some days were warm and sunny, some days damp with heavy mist. Aaron didn't seem to notice. He walked out each morning and returned each night wearing a rain jacket and lugging his briefcase overstuffed with files.

§§§

Clumps of peanuts vanished from the far end of the garden as soon as the stalks were six inches high, the leaves thick and spreading. "Mama," Hami said, "Someone is stealing peanuts still."

Anna told him to dig up a batch nearer the house and replant them where the others disappeared. "Don't forget to rake in some manure," she said.

"Mama, we are feeding a thief," he said.

"That thief must be very hungry," Anna replied. "What should we do, Hami? We have water when others don't. We have seeds and manure and hoes to work the manure into the soil. We have you and Eva and Tobias, too, to hoe and weed and harvest the plants. I know it's not right to encourage a thief, but is it right to have so much when others have so little?"

Hami rubbed his toe against the ground and didn't answer for a while. Finally, he looked down at her, his eyes begging her to understand. "Mama," he said, "none of us would have a house to live in, food to eat, without you and Baba. The GM does not sleep while others are working."

"That's true, Hami. The GM works very hard. What do

153

you think he would do about this thief?"

Hami shook his head. "I do not know, Mama."

Anna didn't know either, but she would soon find out.

§§§

Together, Tobias and Anna created a grocery list to feed visitors arriving from the government and the World Bank. It took two runs to Iringa and one to Mbeya to obtain all they needed for a cocktail party followed by a dinner. Tobias procured a white chef's jacket to wear while serving the cocktail fare: mushroom crescents, tomatoes stuffed with guacamole, deviled eggs, shrimp in puff pastry.

Three of the guests were Americans from the World Bank, one a Greek immigrant, one from Australia and one from Japan. Mr. Saito, the Japanese, was on the patio, talking to Emanuel Chiza, director of personnel, who was sprinkling Japanese words into the conversation. When Anna asked him how he knew Japanese, Chiza said that, for two years, he had studied business at Asia University in Tokyo.

"Was it not difficult to study in Japanese?" she asked.

"The introductory courses were offered in English," Chiza said, "and we had fast immersion courses in Japanese. There are only two public universities even now in Tanzania," he added, "and less than 5,000 students attending. So most of us studied for some time abroad."

He peered through the open door into the living room. "Some fifteen of the managers and mill operators have been sent to the UK to study various aspects of papermaking. Chief Shasani over there—Alan—has a degree in Business and Management from the University of Edinburgh in Scotland."

"What about Mr. Kamala, the horticulturist?" Anna asked.

"He took courses at the University of Greenwich in the UK. One of the best in the world."

"And Mr. Shao?"

Chiza looked down, chewed on his thumb, then looked up. "Some place in the U.S., I think. Florida. No, Texas. He only stayed a short time. Texas Bible—no, something like TC—"

"TCU? Texas Christian University?" Anna asked.

"Yes, that's it." Chiza shook his head, as if he couldn't envision Shao at any university.

"I once considered going there," Anna said.

Chiza looked at her more closely. "Did you go to university, Mrs. Chadwick?"

"I graduated from a small college in Pennsylvania," Anna said.

"What college was that?"

Anna well knew the elitist reputation of the seven sister schools. "Bryn Mawr," she whispered, then quickly added. "I had a scholarship."

"Oh," he said. "I don't think I know that place."

§§§

After the guests left, Anna told Aaron how impressed she was by the level of education his staff had attained in countries which required a command of English or another foreign language.

"And their boss is a lowly English Literature graduate from Yale. Shows you the power of the humanities," he said. "They have worked hard and gained much from their education—though some gained not much more than an imported truck brought into the country on return."

He shook his head. "I didn't mean that. Most of the management deserve better than they are getting. Much better."

Tobias asked if he could stay the night in the servant's quarters. Aaron offered to drive him home. "Sir, the road is rough and hard to see at night. I am okay here."

So Anna helped Tobias load the last of the utensils in the dishwasher, then handed him a stack of sheets, a pillow and a blanket. He wiped off the countertop, turned off the light and left the kitchen for the room out back, empty but for an army cot.

At two in the morning, a scuffle in the garden awoke Anna. She jabbed Aaron, who moved further from her on the bed. She jabbed him again and whispered, "You have to wake up. Something's going on out there."

Aaron sat up, listened, then jumped from the bed and pulled on a pair of jeans. Anna grabbed a robe and stood by the patio door he'd left open. The moon was bright enough to softly light the yard. Aaron switched on the porch light and ran across the patio. "Honey, no!" Anna yelled, but he raced toward the vegetable garden where two men were grappling with each other.

"Aaron, NO!" she yelled again. He was wearing nothing but a pair of jeans. He had no weapon. He was strong, but not strong enough to hold his own against a younger intruder. Still, Aaron ran on, either not hearing her or ignoring her. He was now just a few feet from the two men.

Voices rose, Swahili voices. One was clearly the voice of Tobias. Then the three men were intertwined. The intruder ducked low. Aaron grabbed him by the shoulders. Tobias spoke sharply in Swahili and pushed him to the ground.

From where Anna was standing, it appeared that Aaron and Tobias were holding him down. Next she heard Aaron's voice: "You will leave this place at once and never be seen in

Ahadi again." Aaron stepped back, releasing his grip. Tobias did the same. The intruder rose and, still bent over, turned and fled toward the street.

Now Anna heard laughter—first Aaron, then Tobias. They parted, Tobias heading toward the servants' quarters, Aaron toward the patio.

Aaron came into the house panting, grabbed a corner of Anna's robe and wiped down his neck and chest. "We caught our peanut thief," he said. "Rather, Tobias caught him. Had him in a perfect hammerlock."

"He seemed too small to be the karangaman," Anna said.

"But not too small to be Jonas Shao's cook," Aaron said.

§§§

The next morning, a Saturday, Tobias came into the kitchen with a basket loaded with tomatoes. "I will take you home," Anna said. "Today is your day off. You worked hard last night, and even caught our thief."

Tobias ran his hand through the basket and pleaded with her. "Mama, there are too many ripe tomatoes. They will spoil if I don't make sauce today."

Some of the tomatoes in the basket were still tinged with green, but Anna had learned not to argue with Tobias. He was usually right. He cooked the tomatoes, then he and Anna worked at the sink, filling Ziploc bags that had been washed and reused several times.

"Tobias," she said, "Mrs. Sikes said you should work for a hotel. Is that something you wanted to do?"

He looked at her, alarmed. "Mama, no. Please. Here I have my *shamba*, and your *shamba* to plant, and I can cook many things." He backed away from the sink. "Are you not happy with my work?"

"Tobias, the GM and I are very happy with your work.

We are glad you are here. But what will you do when we leave?"

"I hope you will stay a long time."

Anna smiled. "Thank you, Tobias, but you know that won't happen."

Tobias looked at her, startled. "Mama, you are not leaving soon, are you?"

"Probably not for a while," she said, "but, in the meantime, perhaps you should think about what you will do when the last *mzungu* leaves Tanzania."

"That will be a sad day," he said.

"Maybe it will be a good day," Anna replied. "Because it will mean that the mill is in the hands of your countrymen."

"Maybe, Mama," he said. "But I think it is very difficult to run this mill."

§§§

Mid-morning, Anna convinced Tobias to load his bicycle in the back of the Land Cruiser. He directed her onto a dirt road descending into the valley, then halfway up the next hillside to his house, formed from mud, the roof thatched with straw. A field of maize loomed over the back of the house, and the front garden was crammed with a dozen types of flowers and nearly as many varieties of vegetables. In a second small building which served as the kitchen, there was a large clay pot half filled with water. In the center of the bare floor was a black circle of charcoal residue.

The house had two rooms for five people—Tobias, his wife, Rachel, her mother, a two-year old, Hannah, and Solomon, the six-year-old son of his late brother whom they'd adopted. The sitting room was furnished with lawn chairs, and taped to the wall were pictures from church bulletins and magazines.

A blue *kanga* imprinted with purple and white daisies hung from an expandable rod to block off the bedroom. Anna asked Tobias to translate the words imprinted on the bottom: *Mpaji ni Mungu.*

He bowed his head and folded his hands together as if in prayer. "Mama," he said, "it means that God helps us, feeds us."

A Tanzanian Story

CHAPTER NINETEEN: DOCTOR OGBU

*T*he next morning Becky Barnett stopped by the house to tell Anna that the truck driver, Samir, had succumbed on a cot in his mother's house in Mafinga. She called it what it was: Acquired Immune Deficiency Syndrome.

Becky also dropped off a copy of a recent edition of the *International Herald Tribune*. A story proclaimed that the first words had been posted on the World Wide Web. Anna was reading further to find out what that meant when Grace Kapera appeared at the door. Her eyes reflected sorrow, but she held her head even higher than usual, as if to retain her tears. She told Anna that her sister, Elena, near her delivery time, was bleeding, but Doctor Ogbu said it was nothing and sent her away. "Every footstep was agony as Elena walked down the hill to her home. She has an appointment tomorrow morning for delivery, but I don't think she can make it back up the hill."

"I'll ask Aaron to take the Suzuki to work," Anna said. "We'll take her in the Land Cruiser. What time does the clinic open?"

"At nine, I think," Grace said. "I will come at 8:45 tomorrow morning, and we will fetch my sister."

"No, I will come to your home and pick you up at 8:45," Anna said.

But at 8:15 in the morning a small girl appeared at the door with note from Grace. "There is no need to come today. I will explain later."

161

Anna tried to call Grace but, as usual, the phone wasn't working. She hopped in the Land Cruiser and drove to Grace's home, but nobody answered the door. Anna asked a neighbor where she could find Grace, but the neighbor only smiled. Where, she wondered, growing frantic, were the words she needed? Home —*Nyumbani*. Sister—Anna had no clue. Why hadn't she been more aggressive in finding a tutor to teach her Swahili?

"Sister, Elena, *nyumbani,*" she said to the neighbor. Again, the woman only smiled.

Anna sped to the clinic, but it was closed. She realized she was wasting time and went to the school where she found Marianna Monyo, the assistant headmistress, and asked for Grace.

"She sent a child with a message that she will not be at school today," Marianna said. "That is very strange for Grace."

Marianna told Anna where Grace's sister lived. Anna ran to the car and turned into the lowest street on the hillside, where houses were small and close together. She knocked on the next to last door, called out "*Hodi, Hodi,*" and Grace appeared. From inside, Anna heard a woman's voice, low-pitched, moaning.

"Oh, Anna. I am glad to see you. I sent a message because I couldn't leave my sister."

Grace told Anna that her sister was beginning to deliver the baby the night before. They sent for Doctor Ogbu, but he wasn't at the clinic or at home. She hesitated, swallowed, spoke more slowly.

"So I sent for a woman who is called a midwife, but she arrived late. By then, the baby—"

Grace held her head high, but couldn't retain the single

tear that ran down her cheek. "The silence when the baby came—I still hear it—the sound of no one being inside that tiny boy."

§§§

Anna was furious. She hugged Grace, then went directly to the mill to tell Aaron what had happened. He shut the door to his office and walked in circles around his desk. The more he paced, the angrier he appeared. "Dammit!" He pushed the hair back from his brow, shook his head. His hair flopped back down across his eyes. He rubbed the back of his neck. His hair was tangled, drooping over the frayed collar of his white dress shirt.

Anna sighed. "You need a haircut," she said.

"I need a new doctor on site," he said, his voice rising. "Emanuel Chiza has told me the reason Doctor Ogbu is gone so often is that he maintains a pharmacy in Dar Es Salaam. Chiza also hinted that Ogbu does his own purchasing from cash advances and swaps outdated drugs from his store with drugs for the mill. If the dispensary is out of a drug—as it often is—the patient is told to go see the doctor at home. He will supply what they need at a hefty price. I want to fire the bastard, but the government says there is no replacement for him."

Aaron stopped pacing and ran both hands brusquely through his hair. "You're right," he said, his voice quieter. "I need a haircut. Maybe a barber on site would be more effective than this so-called doctor."

But immediately his voice rose again. "The guy's not even Tanzanian. He's from Nigeria. So I can't help but wonder how he managed to land a job at a government-owned project." Aaron swallowed, shook his head.

"At least he has *some* command of Swahili. Enough,

at least, to converse regularly with our crafty CFO, Jonas Shao. And Shao must be tight with someone in finance at the ministry. I'm almost sure of it."

He sat at his desk, twirled the chair around, then faced Anna again. "And do you remember Shao's cook?"

"Didn't you banish him when he stole our peanuts?" Anna asked.

"He's still here and just got another raise. He's Shao's wife's youngest brother."

§§§

Aaron came through the door at 6:30 in the evening, shaking his head. He dropped his briefcase beside the computer in the back bedroom, poured his evening scotch and slumped across the loveseat in the sitting room.

"Right after you came to the office, I called a meeting of my five top managers to discuss what we knew about Dr. Ogbu. Then I drew up a list of complaints for Ogbu to sign. I sent Emmanuel Chiza off to find Ogbu. He was at the Bwana Club swigging down a beer. So I called the managers back together, brought Ogbu into the room, read him the list of complaints and told him he had three days to reply."

Aaron sat up and took a hefty swig of his scotch. "But, would you believe, the doctor showed up in my office this afternoon."

"'I've just now joined the church,' he said. 'So there is no need to respond to these charges.'"

"And you said?"

Aaron's eyes turned playful. "I told him that, since he had joined the church, I expected his response to be honest—and thorough."

§§§

The mill ran sporadically. In a few weeks, the last American expatriates—except for Aaron—would leave their jobs. The management contract was due to be renewed the first of the year, and Aaron had already lined up potential replacements with people he had met in his travels: a mill manager from Mumbai, India, a training manager from Gwadar, Pakistan, and a pulp mill manager from Nairobi, Kenya.

Aaron told Anna that, because of government debt, and in keeping with their new directive to privatize parastatal industries, two Indian firms had submitted letters of intent to purchase the mill. "If the government accepts a bid, the contract won't be renewed, and we'll probably be leaving around the first of February".

"How come the Barnetts and Fullers are leaving before Christmas?" Anna asked.

"They used accumulated vacation time."

"Do we have any of that?"

Aaron laughed and gave her a hug. "Aaron, look at me," she said. He lowered his head, looked into her eyes. "What if the contract isn't renewed?" she asked.

"Didn't you once tell me you wanted to go to Indonesia?"

"Aaron! No way!"

He hugged her again. "Okay, then. For you, Anna, and for the good of Ahadi, we'll get the contract signed."

A Tanzanian Story

CHAPTER TWENTY: HAMI'S PROBLEM

*T*here was a knock on the door, and Layla, the attractive young woman who cooked and cleaned for Ryder McGowan, asked if she could come in. She was wearing a bright violet *kanga* over a white jersey, and the straps of her gold high-heel sandals wound around her ankles. She bowed her head. "Please, may I speak in private with the GM?" she asked.

Anna called Aaron to the door and went into the kitchen to make breakfast. Fifteen minutes later, she heard the door shut, and Aaron was walking through the living room. He cried out, "Oh, shit!" and headed down the hallway.

Anna found him with his head buried in his hands against the window bars in the bedroom. "She's pregnant," he said. "The conversation was a little round-about, but Ryder McGowan, that SOB, is in some way responsible. And Shao appears to be involved. Can you believe that Eric Sikes was going to extend McGowan's contract?"

"Has McGowan been seen since he cleared out his house?"

Aaron turned around and pushed the hair from his forehead. "I hear he's in Dar Es Salaam. Evidently he was seen at the breakfast bar at the Kilimanjaro Hotel conferring with a British group hoping to build a luxury hotel in Zanzibar."

§§§

Though it was a Saturday, Aaron left for the mill, saying he would return before lunch, then he and Anna would go to Mbeya to shop. Mid-morning, Anna stepped out onto the patio to find Hami sitting on the bench in the thinking garden. Normally, when Anna approached, he jumped up and greeted her, but today he remained on the bench, apparently thinking.

"*Jambo*, Hami," she said.

He looked up, startled, but didn't rise. "*Jambo*, Mama. *Habari?*"

"*Nzuri*. Are you okay?" she asked. "It's your day off, but you are here."

"I came here to think because I have a big problem, Mama," he said.

"Would you like to tell me about this problem?" He hesitated, rubbed his hands together, then nodded. Anna suggested that they both sit at the table on the patio to talk.

As Anna suspected, Hami was in love. With Eva. And, as she also suspected, Eva was in love with Hami. The problem was that Hami was Muslim, and Eva was Christian, having been baptized by Methodist missionaries as a ten-year-old child.

"Eva's parents, they are okay with me," Hami said. "They had her baptized, but didn't ever join the church. It is my father who is causing my big problem." Hami smacked his fist against his thigh.

"He says I should not marry outside the faith, though many men of Islam do that very thing. Mama, it is true."

He told Anna that a cousin, a son of his mother's brother, married a Christian and was no longer welcome in his family's home. "They moved to another village, far away, as if dead to the family. I could not live that way."

"What does your Imam say?"

Hami grinned. "Mama, do you see a mosque in Ahadi?"

"Where does your father live? Is there a mosque nearby?"

"No, Mama. He is the chief in a small village past the valley, forty kilometers over there." Hami pointed beyond the banana tree. "My father raises many chickens and grows maize."

"Your uncle, Mahib Kamala, the horticulturist, is he not your father's brother?"

"Yes, Mama. He is my father's brother. He is a smart man."

"And what does he say?"

"He only says that Eva is a very pretty girl."

"And what does Tobias say?"

"He says I should convert to Baptist like him. Oh, then my father would be even more angry."

"Tell me, Hami," she said. "How long have you loved Eva?"

"It has been a long time," he said. "Eva came to work in the garden, and she worked very hard. But one day, after two months, Eva and I were standing over there by the bush house when Mama Sikes, she call to Eva and say she must leave this place. I don't understand why it is. After that, we did not see each other for some time."

Hami looked down at the table. His voice was soft, pleading. "Mama, I want to marry."

§§§

On Monday morning Eva ran to Anna. "Come, Mama, look!" They stepped outside the back door. "Look, Mama, the mill is making beautiful clouds!" Anna could see the top of the towers, the smoke flowing out, curling into huge white puffs, very much like clouds.

"Stay here," Anna said. "I'll bring my camera, and you can take pictures of these clouds. When we develop them, you can give a picture to the GM. It will make him very happy."

169

Anna retrieved her camera, loaded with black and white film. She put a polarizing filter on the lens to darken the sky and enhance the billowing smoke. Then she showed Eva how to zoom in and out. "Push the button when the picture looks good to you." Eva took a picture.

"Hold the camera very still," Anna said. Eva took another picture.

"I think that one is better," Eva said.

"Okay, now turn the ring left to take a picture of all the clouds you can see." Eva fiddled with the zoom, then snapped the shutter again.

"As soon as I finish this roll of film, we can develop the pictures," Anna said.

"I hope that will be soon, Mama," Eva said.

"There are only a few shots left. Why don't I take some pictures of you?"

Eva stood stiff, unsmiling.

"No," Anna said and picked a blossom from a nearby bougainvillea. "Hold this flower in your hand and look at it as if it is a gift from a good friend."

Eva looked down at the flower as if it were a treasure, and Anna moved around to photograph the flower and Eva's appreciative eyes. When the roll of film was finished, Anna started to go inside, but Eva said she had something to tell her. They sat at the patio table.

"Hami has given me a Quran written in Swahili, and I have been studying the words. There is much I cannot understand," she said. "But some of the words speak well. Allah says, 'Seek help in patience and prayer.' I am seeking that help.

"Hami says his father feels it is better for him to choose Hami's wife, and it should be someone Hami doesn't know.

That is the way it is done."

Then she spoke even more carefully, as if trying to find the exact words. "But the Quran says: 'When something is created as one part of two things, it is not a whole thing without the other.' I think Allah means Hami and I should marry."

Anna told her that she understood her interpretation. How often, when Aaron was traveling, had she felt as if part of her were missing.

"Hami says if I can believe, I can convert, and his father may agree to the marrying if I be pure. She looked at Anna, her eyes pleading. "Hami and I have never— Mama, Hami knows—"

"Oh, Eva," Anna said. "This is very difficult."

As much as Anna wanted to see Eva and Hami happy, she felt she didn't understand enough about the challenges they would encounter—and not only from their families—to offer good advice. "Your problem reminds me of a wise proverb I heard the other day," she said. "What do you know about a river from bathing in the stream that feeds it?"

Eva pondered the question. "I understand what you say. I am learning much already," she said. "But, Mama, there is so much to know. I am afraid to make a mistake."

"I think reading the Quran is a start, but there is much more to consider. Why don't you and I go visit Jabari's wife? Maybe she can tell you what you need to know. Maybe she can guide you."

Eva brightened. "Oh, yes, Mama. That is a most excellent idea. I know it is wrong to say you believe if you do not. Maybe she can help me believe so Hami and I can become the whole thing."

Jabari's wife, Dafina, welcomed them. Anna sat patiently

on the one chair in their small sitting room while Dafina and Eva sat on a cot draped with a blue *kanga* bordered with elephants. In the far corner of the cot, Anna saw a tuft of purple yarn—Johani's doll. She was startled. She thought she must be wrong, but no, what else could it be?

She imagined Johani running through the room, jumping on the cot, grabbing the doll and running out again. Anna held her head in her hands, wanting nothing more than to leave, to step outside and breathe deeply, to think, to heal, to erase her thoughts, too many thoughts, too much sorrow.

But she stayed in the room while Dafina and Eva conversed in Swahili, both of them serious, earnest. As they walked home, Eva told Anna that Dafina had promised she would tell her what she needed to know about Islam. "And if I sincerely want to be Muslim, she will help me declare the faith." Eva twirled down the street.

"Mama GM, this has been a very good day. Thank you."

That night Anna dreamed of a little girl, her purple hair flying behind her as she soared in and out of white, billowing clouds. In her dream, she became that girl, pushed east then west, legs flailing, trying to find a secure place to land.

Like a Mask Dancing

CHAPTER TWENTY-ONE:
AHADI CHRISTMAS BUBBLE

*L*arge bags of rice and cases of Coca-Cola began to arrive in the market, a reminder that Christmas was only three weeks away. And container cars, each twenty feet long, appeared in the Barnett and Fuller driveways.

Anna was beginning to feel homesick. She missed Christopher, Murray, her in-laws and her mother. She missed the toy nutcrackers marching up their staircase, the holly wreath on the door, candles in each window. She missed the mistletoe ball hanging from the chandelier in the entrance hall, the six-foot live balsam fir bowed down with ornaments collected over the years. She missed her neighbors, her friends from the board of the Windsor Craft Store and Lebanon College. She longed for outdoor lights reflected in white pines. She even felt a craving for knee-deep snow.

So she wrote a gloomy Christmas letter and mailed it to everyone on their address list.

Merry Christmas from Ahadi, Tanzania
December 15, 1990

Plenty of church bells, lots of eucalyptus and red pine in the paper mill forests, poinsettia trees six feet tall, but not much in the way of jingle bells. Not one frosted nose. If Santa comes, it's likely to be on a rhinoceros.

Only God, the World Bank and the Tanzanian government know why they dropped this mill into a valley in the middle

173

of nowhere when the millions spent (by Canada, Sweden, your tax dollars) might have irrigated dry lands or upgraded farm production and staved off the inevitable drought.

The daily problems—money, fuel, transportation, spare parts—are seemingly insurmountable, but Aaron remains optimistic and has already made remarkable progress.

We live at the top of a hill in a town built at the end of the world's longest gravel road. Our house overlooks the mill and mill houses, a valley and imposing escarpment. Surrounding us are small villages of thatched-roof mud huts. The local market has fifteen stalls, half of them closed, where you can buy tomatoes, bananas, dried fish and soap powder. To buy more useful staples you drive ten hours without stopping to Dar Es Salaam. We often do.

Tanzania is at the bottom of the list for per capita income and industrialization, but it's a country rich in land, untapped resources and big-game reserves. We have spent time among elephants, monkeys, zebras, giraffes, lions. The mountains are spectacular; the people warm, good-humored. Everyone owns a hoe. In these nine months, traversing thousands of kilometers, I've seen maybe four tractors. Baskets, pots, furniture, toys—what few there are—are made by hand. Travel is on foot. Every day is the same as the day before, boredom relieved by birth, weddings, death—and church or Muslim prayer services. Aaron says that the Long-Range Planning Manager has three Bibles on his desk but no forecast spreadsheets.

We are well. Yellow fever shots, malaria pills and boiled, filtered water immunize us from tropical diseases. I tend (with the help of a gardener) a two-acre flower and vegetable shamba; teach a little; take pictures when I'm not cooking or am too overwhelmed by thoughts and feelings about Africa.

Like a Mask Dancing

*We look forward to hearing from you, though with phones
and mail being what they are here, a thousand kilometers
from the end of the earth, we will wait patiently and hope
Christmas arrives by Easter.*

*By the way, the stars at night are nothing less than awe-
inspiring.*

§§§

To prepare for a going-away cocktail party for the expatriates,
Tobias baked a cake and slathered it with chocolate icing,
then added sprigs of parsley and small blue orchids. In
blue icing across the cake, he wrote *kwaheri*—goodbye. "I
think," he told Anna, "if it happens that no *wazungus* be left
in Ahadi, I will open a cake bakery."

"That sounds like a good idea," Anna said, "but will you
be able to sell enough cakes in Ahadi? You should test the
idea while you still work here. Bake cakes as well as bread
to sell."

Tobias' eyes lit up. "I think that is a very good idea," he
said.

Tobias served chicken salad in puff pastry, home-made
cheese biscuits, home-made potato chips with onion dip
created from home-made cottage cheese. Priscilla brought
along a plate of Ritz crackers.

And, by noon the next day, Aaron and Anna were the
only *wazungus* in Ahadi.

§§§

As soon as school was dismissed for the holidays, Anna
invited Grace Kapera and the assistant head mistress,
Marianna Monyo, to the house to make food and decorations.

The first morning they knocked timidly on the door.
Anna told Eva Pengo to stop ironing so she could join them,
and all of them took seats at the dining room table to begin

to cut out cookies. Marianna named each gingerbread boy Joseph. The animals were manger pigs and manger chickens. As they put the cookies in the oven to bake, they sang, off key, in English and Swahili: *Joy to the World, Furaha Kwa Ulimwengu.*

While braiding wreaths of frangipani, pine and eucalyptus, they ate breaded eggplant and drank iced lime sodas. They laughed and sang, *Oh, Come All Ye Faithful.*

Grace and Marianna asked if they could return the next day and walked down the hill singing *Mjini Bethlehemu.*The next day they baked again, then braided more wreaths and filled containers with lilies and roses.

Aaron came home from work early, and he and Anna drove down to the pulpwood forest where they dug up a scraggly pine growing among the eucalyptus. As they were loading it into the back of the Land Cruiser, a band of six hunters, each with a dog, came out of the forest, spears over their shoulders, the head, tail end or torso of a wild boar hanging from each spear. The dogs were circling the men, eyeing the boars and barking loudly. Aaron and Anna jumped into the car, but Aaron realized he'd left the key dangling from the rear lock. They waited in the car by the side of the road until the hunters crossed in front of them, waved and disappeared down another path.

"I'm glad they didn't ask us for a *lifti*," Aaron said. They both laughed. Anna took his wrist from the steering wheel and rubbed his hand across her lips. "You are the most amazing man," she said.

"And that's my reward for leaving the key in the boot?" he said.

She laughed again. Aaron waited another minute, then leapt from the car and quickly retrieved the key. When they got home, he planted the little pine in a plastic bucket and anchored it with stones from the thinking garden. He put it in front of the window beside the carving of the old man and his dog. Simba circled the tree, then, apparently not impressed, retreated to her dish in the kitchen.

The next morning, the third day of Christmas preparations, Grace and Marianna arrived five minutes early. They'd brought Grace's sister, Elena, who appeared to be growing stronger after the loss of her baby. They called out *"hodi, hodi,"* and Eva opened the door before they'd even had a chance to knock. Together they decorated the pine with a pair of rhinestone earrings, one red sock, gingerbread Josephs, strips of wrapping paper. Grace blessed it with a long prayer. Elena added an extra amen.

Just before noon, Jabari arrived and unloaded fifty half-pound bags of rice. "This is very good rice, Mama," he said. "It has been sifted and washed, so it is very clean."

"Where did you get it?" Anna asked.

"Mr. Chadwick sent me this morning to Mbeya. He said you and the ladies were going to distribute gifts within the village. This is the finest rice, which everyone will appreciate very much."

Anna thought about the Christmases when she had struggled to find the right gifts for her mother, other family members, her friends. She thought about how she had overspent and wondered if the gifts really meant anything to the recipients. And here she was with fifty small bags of rice for Christmas gifts—modest gifts which Jabari had just assured her would be valued.

"Jabari—you have no idea how much—" She breathed deeply, choked down her emotion. "Jabari," she said. "You are a very good man. Thank you. We will make sure they are delivered."

In the dining room, she joined Grace, Mariana, Elena and Eva who were again singing *Furaha Kwa Ulimwengu*, and every word rang out in four separate but joyous keys. They smothered cupcakes with pink and turquoise icing, lettuce leaves, hibiscus, candied cherries, tasted two each and put the rest aside to deliver, along with the cookies and fifty bags of clean, white rice, to village churches, mill workers, neighbors—whether Christian or Muslim. They all left the house together, singing *Sisi Kings Tatu—We Three Kings of Orient Are.* And, surprisingly to Anna, they were welcomed with smiles and thanks at every door. It seemed to make no difference that this was a Christian celebration. Any reason to celebrate was reason enough.

Anna was no longer homesick. In fact, she felt more of the magic of Christmas than she had felt since she was a child.

§§§

Anna hung small baskets over the fireplace to fill with gifts she and Aaron found for each other. On Aaron's, she used a black magic marker to write *GM*, and, on hers, *MAMA GM.* A half a dozen wrapped gifts which arrived in the mail from family and friends were spread under the tree.

Anna and Eva worked together in the darkroom, and Eva printed a photograph of the clouds billowing out from the smokestacks. She said she wanted to take the picture with her for just two days and then would bring it back to give to the GM. When she returned two days before Christmas, it was bordered by a mat painted powder blue and placed in a simple white frame.

"The frame is beautiful!" Anna said. "Who did this for you?"

"I made this from a packing box," Eva said, tracing her finger around the mat. "My cousin is a carpenter. He did the rest." She lowered her head. "I hope it is good enough. Do you think the GM will like it?"

"The GM will love it!" Anna said. "Can you bring it tonight when he comes home from work and give it to him then?"

Her eyes sparkled. "I will come tonight, Mama."

Aaron had been home for an hour, but Eva hadn't appeared. Anna put dinner on the table, and they were just sitting down to eat when there was a knock on the door. Aaron rose from the table and grumbled, "What now?"

When he returned to the table, he was carrying the framed picture and biting his lip, as if to hold back emotion.

"I'm going to hang this over my desk," he said, "for inspiration. What a perfect Christmas gift." He placed the picture against the candlestick at the far end of the table so it faced them both, and he examined it from time to time as they ate. As he rose to carry his plate to the kitchen, he looked at it once more, then at Anna. "You know, you have brought out the best in that young woman."

Anna smiled. "I think she's better at taking pictures than ironing your jockey shorts."

§§§

On Christmas Eve they joined a packed congregation for the pageant at the Methodist Church, the largest church in Ahadi. Harrod, a young woman in a security guard uniform, clutched the pillow enlarging her belly—a sign of wealth—as she raced down the aisle, fanned by a tall attendant waving a palm. She chased Joseph and Mary who carried a white baby doll to the crib beside the pulpit. At one point, the baby slipped from Mary's hand, but Joseph caught it. The congregation clapped.

A Wiseman in a turban and sheet turned on a flashlight and a star appeared—as did a live goat which a shepherd, dressed as a Maasai, tied to the manger. The goat bleated loudly as the choir sang Christmas carols a cappella in Swahili, and, despite the goat, the music was stirring.

At the end of the service, a dozen children in white robes, faces shy and frightened, walked onto the stage to sing the Tanzanian national anthem. *Bless us, Children of Africa.*

The audience clapped for a long time. Aaron and Anna clapped the loudest.

The children raced from the church, their high voices excited. Their parents seemed subdued, even solemn. As they turned into their streets, they wished Aaron and Anna a merry Christmas: *"Krismasi ya furaha."*

"Krismasi ya furaha," Anna and Aaron replied.

They arrived home at 8:15 that night, and Anna dashed to the phone to call Christopher.

It would be just after noon, Christmas Eve, in Vermont. Miraculously, the call went through. Just as miraculously, Christopher was off for the day and had just come in from walking Murray.

"Krismasi ya furaha," Anna said.

"Hey there—same to you, Mom."

"Did you get our Christmas package?"

"Not yet," he said, "but there's still half a day left for delivery."

"I'm sorry, Christopher. I mailed it nearly a month ago."

"It's okay, Mom," he said.

But, to Anna, it was not okay. This was the first time they hadn't celebrated Christmas together. "You have no idea how much I miss you," she said.

"It's okay, Mom. Really," he said, paused then added, "But you know what? I miss you, too."

"What are you doing tomorrow?"

"I'm going to ask Beryl to marry me. Then—"

"Christopher! Really?"

He laughed. "No, mom. Just kidding. We're going to the Rothchild's house for lunch, then skiing at Mount Ascutney."

"Christopher, I love you. I wish—you would really like it here." Anna felt tears welling up in her eyes. "Your dad wants to talk to you."

She handed the phone to Aaron. "Hey, Critter. How you doing?"

Anna listened to Aaron's side of the conversation, interspersed by silences. "Hmmnn….not bad…Wow! That's great…Absolutely….whatever you think…I'm proud of you, son."

After a long pause, Aaron said, "So, do you think you could put Murray on the line?" Anna laughed and stole the phone from him. "We'll try to call tomorrow," she said. "We love you. Merry Christmas."

"I love you too, Mom, and—" The line went dead.

§§§

When they arose on Christmas morning, the sky was dark over the valley, and darkened more by the time they finished breakfast. Since there weren't a lot of gifts to unwrap, and they had no plans for the day, they delayed the process as long as possible.

Anna turned on the little portable tape player she'd sent in their air shipment and put in a cassette of Bach's Brandenburg Concertos Four, Five and Six, not exactly Christmas music, but both joyous and meditative, so close enough.

The gifts were perfect: raisins, Snickers bars, socks and

Ziploc bags. Aaron gave Anna a large, square Tanzanite stone purchased from a jeweler in Dar Es Salaam. She gave him a pair of Nikon binoculars she'd convinced the Barnetts to sell her before they left. She also gave him a carved warthog—flawless down to the tusks, the wart-like protrusions, large testicles, tiny eyes and skinny tail.

He turned the warthog in his hand and leaned over to kiss her. "It's perfect. Thank you," he said.

She knew it wasn't perfect, but it was the best she could do.

Anna was putting together a small Christmas feast when lightning pulsed through the yard. A thwack of thunder, then another. More lightning. The music suddenly stopped. She flinched and ran to the window. The wind was twisting the trees in the garden, bending the hedges, toppling flowers and vegetables, and rain was blowing sideways across the yard. The bronze sunbird tumbled over, its beak stabbing the ground. She grabbed the camera, loaded it with the fastest film she had, and was trying to capture this furious storm through the bars on the back window when Aaron emerged from the hallway carrying a floppy disk. "The hard drive on the laptop is fried. So is the printer."

§§§

He spent the next hour with a screwdriver extracting the hard drive from the computer. He said he'd get word to Howard Hammond to bring a replacement when he came for the management contract meeting after the new year.

Anna tried to figure out how to salvage the late afternoon meal. The roast beef was on the raw side of rare; the potatoes were mashed but still cold; the green beans frozen. The rain was blowing so hard through the breezeway and across the patio there was no place to put the grill.

182

She took some left-over lemon chicken and a half cup of chicken stock from the refrigerator, mixed it in a baking pan, stirred in the green beans and topped it with the potatoes and a dollop of butter. She took the grate from the roasting pan, placed it in front of the fire in the fireplace and laid the pan on top, then squatted in front of the hearth, stirring the mixture and turning the pan until it was warm enough to serve. She added some parsley, shredded some cheese on top, lit candles in the dining room and told Aaron dinner was ready.

"It's called Ahadi Christmas Bubble," she told him. "It's not what I planned, but hopefully not half bad." And, actually, it wasn't half bad, but not quite three-quarters good, either.

After they ate, Aaron started to get up, but Anna told him to stay put for dessert. She poured a half cup of 90-proof brandy over the Christmas pudding Tobias and she had been concocting for a month—more oranges than raisins, mangos rather than plums—lit it with a match and carried it, flaming, into the dining room.

The lights flickered on. The music resumed. They lifted their forks. The lights went out and the music stopped. They dug in. The pudding was good enough to make up for the Ahadi Christmas Bubble.

Anna wanted to call Christopher again, but when she lifted the receiver there was no dial tone.

In bed that night they held each other closely, more closely with each thunderclap. When they awoke in the morning, they were interlaced, husband and wife, coupled together, the man within the woman, the man she had been willing to follow to Africa; the man she loved beyond all she had ever understood about love.

A Tanzanian Story

CHAPTER TWENTY-TWO: CRISIS

*E*arly Wednesday, as they ate a bowl of Weetabix and drank instant coffee heated on the grill, Anna asked Aaron if they might leave Sunday for a two-day New Year's trip to Ruaha National Park, a half-day's drive north from Ahadi. "There are a lot of elephants, and the birds are supposed to be spectacular, but I'm hoping for a cheetah."

"Great idea," Aaron said. "We could both use a change of scenery, and with my computer dead, there's less I can accomplish here."

He grew more animated as he planned the trip. "I'll have maintenance perform a good checkup on the Land Cruiser. We'll leave Jabari here for some well-deserved time off. The woodlands director is from that area. I'll ask him for the best route to take." Aaron rose from the table smiling, and an hour later the power returned.

§§§

Friday, mid-morning, Tobias had finished preparations for lunch. A chicken stew simmered on the stove, and a small angel food cake was rising in the oven.

Tobias told Anna that the cake was for an upcoming wedding. Anna asked him how many were attending. "Maybe a hundred," he answered. "The cake is only for the *firsti* table. If there is any left over, the others can have small crumbs."

"Oh, Tobias," Anna said. "You could have made a bigger cake."

"No. That's all they could afford."

She had contributed the oven, the flour, egg whites and sugar, but Tobias had done the work, and was obviously charging for that work. Perhaps he was becoming a shrewd businessman.

Anna left for the darkroom, passing through the living room where Eva danced the mop across floor to Strauss's Blue Danube Waltz. The music ended in the middle of a slur, and Eva slid to a halt.

Tobias later emerged from the kitchen, a dish cloth and wooden spoon in his hand. "No power, Mama," he said.

"But your cake," Anna said.

Tobias grimaced. "It has fallen down," he said.

"Scrape the icing off the leftover Christmas cupcakes still in the freezer," Anna said.

"They're probably half thawed out by now. Arrange them tight together in the largest baking pan, flatten them down and fill the cracks with icing. Then ice them again using colors that are right for the wedding."

An hour later Tobias showed Anna the resurrected cake still in the pan. The icing was light yellow, and a large red hibiscus sagged across the center.

"It looks good," Anna said. "But I don't think you should try to move it onto a plate. Just make sure they return the pan after the wedding."

A few minutes later Jabari arrived with a message from Aaron saying he wouldn't be home for lunch. Aaron showed up at 2:30, nearly dragging his briefcase through the door.

"Everything is gone," he said. "This isn't a power failure. The electricity has been cut off. Totally."

He poked his head into the kitchen, asked Tobias to heat some water for coffee on the grill, then sank into the loveseat.

"We had enough fuel to keep the diesel generator pumping

water up the hill from the river to the mill to avoid sewage backup, but the generator's stopped running. There's only the smaller generator which pumps water up to the townsite. I had the electrical crew haul it to the dispensary, so they can sterilize needles and have lights during the day. They'll haul it back tonight to pump water to the houses, then take it back to the dispensary in the morning. We're down to a 24-hour supply of coal. I have a feeling the national bank has shut down our overdraft, so I called Chief Shasani."

"And he said?"

"His secretary said he was on holiday and wasn't expected back until Wednesday." Aaron dropped his head into his hands, rubbed his forehead then looked up at Anna.

"On top of that, I just discovered that the week before Christmas, Shao signed off on and paid for full loads of limestone and clay, though only half of each were shipped."

Tobias brought Aaron his cup of coffee and a plate of limp, thawed-out peanut butter cookies. Aaron picked up a cookie which broke in half when he tried to lift it to his mouth. He shrugged, ate the half and pushed the plate aside.

"Honey, I'm sorry," he said. "We'll have to postpone the trip to Ruaha. I want to be here during this crisis. Jonas Shao is in Dar now, but won't be able to see anyone until Monday morning. Tuesday is New Year's, so everything will be closed. Also, before the power died this morning, I received a telex confirming that Howard Hammond and a small contingent from New York will be flying in early Wednesday morning for the contract meetings on Thursday, so I'll have to go to Dar on New Year's Day. You, too—presuming you want to come with me."

Anna sat down beside him and leaned against his shoulder. "That sounds like a significantly better deal than staying here, listening to ice cubes melting and water boiling on the grill."

After Aaron downed his coffee and returned to the mill, Anna drove the Suzuki down to the market. There were no candles left, but she bought a couple of kerosene lanterns and three bags of salt. There were still small pyramids of charcoal for sale, but since they had enough to last a week, she left the nuggets for others who had less.

On the way back, three women were trudging up the hill, shouldering large baskets. She loaded the women into the Suzuki, dropped them off at their houses and headed home. She and Tobias filled every pot with water and shoved all that would fit onto the grill to boil it for cooking and cleaning. Then they soaked all the uncooked meat in salt brine, and that evening Aaron loaded the Land Cruiser with packages of melting food from the freezer, plus excess vegetables from the garden—beans, tomatoes, peppers and chard—and took the food to the cafeteria to distribute to the workers.

During the night electricity returned to the townsite but not the mill.

§§§

On New Year's morning, as Aaron and Anna were getting ready to leave for Dar, Jonas Shao stopped by the house to report that, with the help of God, he had made great progress with Tanesco. The electricity was guaranteed to the townsite for the next seven days.

"And the mill?"

Shao shrugged. "First much money must be paid."

"How much are we in arrears?"

"I have the documents in my briefcase at home," he said.

"It will be helpful," said Aaron, "if you will bring them to me now before I leave to meet with the ministry."

After Shao left, Anna turned to Aaron. She was having a hard time believing that the project was salvageable and wondered why Aaron hadn't given up by now.

"So," she said. "We're a government project supported by government funds, but the government bank doesn't issue those funds, and the government-owned power company isn't being paid. Have I got that right?"

"That's pretty much it," Aaron said. "Plus, the finance director appears to be in cahoots with some of our suppliers. Let's go see what we can do about it."

Shao returned with the documents fifteen minutes later, and they finished packing for the trip. But, as Aaron was carrying his hanging bag out the front door, he stopped suddenly and turned back, his eyes closed, his face visibly ashen. He dropped his bag.

"What is it?" Anna ran to him. "Don't look," he said, grabbed her and turned her away from the door. But she did look over her shoulder and saw a mass of white feathers strewn across the stoop, a pair of orange webbed feet sticking up in the air.

Just then Jabari arrived from having filled the Land Cruiser with gas. He stepped out of the car, looked at the steps, backed away, his eyes revealing shock.

Aaron pulled Anna away from the door. He said they needed to talk and led her to the bedroom.

"Come, sit on the bed." he said. "What's happened is serious. Someone has left us a message in the form of a beheaded chicken. It's a Voodoo, black magic kind of thing. It means someone wants us gone."

"As in dead?" Anna asked.

Aaron shook his head. "I don't believe we're in mortal danger, but it's a good thing we'll be away for a while.

Someone is just very unhappy and has decided I am to blame."

He held her by the shoulders, looked into her eyes. "What I want you to do is to stay right here. I'll take your suitcase out and clean up the mess. Then I'll come get you."

But Anna followed Aaron to the front door. The bird was gone. Only a single feather lay in the dirt next to the bottom step.

Jabari ran up to the door and took Anna's suitcase from Aaron.

"Jabari—where did that thing go?" Anna asked.

"I think, Mama, it flew away somewhere," he said, wiping his hands on his pants.

"Jabari, I think it was some kind of warning. Maybe serious," she said.

He lifted her suitcase onto his head. "Don't worry. Mama. It was only a joke."

"If it was a joke, it was a very bad joke," she said.

Jabari put the suitcase in the boot and nodded solemnly. "Yes, Mama. It was a very bad joke."

PART THREE

Uvumilivu unaweza kupika jiwe
Patience can Cook a Stone

January through April 1991

CHAPTER TWENTY-THREE: A PROPOSITION

*A*s they entered the city, Anna, who was sprawled across the back seat of the Land Cruiser, shielded her eyes from flashes of the dazzling sun descending between the buildings. The car swerved, braked suddenly, then accelerated. Anna sat up quickly. "What was that?" she asked.

"Only a headless chicken crossing the road," Aaron said.

"Aaron!" Anna encircled his neck with her hands. He laughed. Jabari looked at her in the rear-view mirror, clearly alarmed.

"It's no joke," she said.

"Mama GM, it was a rooster," Jabari said. "But he was wearing his head."

§§§

It was dark when they checked into the Kilimanjaro hotel. Around 1:00 in the morning, CEO Howard Hammond and the contingent from Transnational Development were to arrive on a flight from New York via Paris. With him were Caleb Weatherly, a company lawyer, financial officer Nick

191

Icovino and Carina Sorenstam. Since Aaron planned to spend much of the day meeting with them at the hotel, Anna would have the use of Jabari and the car. She decided that she and Jabari needed a cultural infusion, a reprieve from thoughts of chickens, whether headless or wearing their heads.

Jabari drove first to Oyster Bay to find the artists who sold Tingatinga paintings created on paper, cloth and pots. Anna liked the intense colors, the juxtaposition of multiple images. People were painted red, brown, green. Fanciful animals—cobalt blue elephants, scarlet giraffes, multicolored toucans—struck impossible poses. She bought a small orange pot painted with black, white and yellow colobus monkeys, each a different size, each gazing off into a different direction. Their tails formed intertwining branches around the base of the pot.

Next, they traveled through the heart of the city to an alley behind a busy market where Jabari told Anna they would find the best wood carvers. In the first stall were a half dozen pieces of intricate Makonde art. Anna took pictures of the artist chipping away at a block of wood with an adze while Jabari inspected the display of finished work, turning the sculptures right and left and asking question after question. He seemed most intrigued by the large ebony tree of life sculpture, a family of smooth, polished figures juxtaposed against each other, some upright, some prone, some at an angle, some carrying water gourds, some with water pots nestled on top of their heads.

The walls of the next stall were jammed with masks, predominately tough masculine faces with large, assertive mouths, many with deeply carved tribal scars, one with a bashed-in nose. Mixed in were long, delicate female faces, several with eyes half closed. A couple of the faces appeared to be sleeping, and Anna wondered if they might not represent the dead. Some of the faces were painted; some were decorated with beads, tufts of hair or strands of woven cloth, and they displayed an enormous range of emotion: joy, sorrow, wonder.

In the next stall they found an assortment of animal masks—kudus, lions, a large elephant, a tiny bat-eared fox with enormous ears. On the center post, a roughly carved mask with rabbit ears and two large rabbit teeth blended into a wide-eyed, astonished human face. Jabari looked at the rabbit mask and smiled. Anna hadn't seen him this light-hearted since Johani died.

The carver, who appeared to be in his mid-thirties, sat on a cushion just inside the stall. His upturned face was hopeful. He said that the rabbit mask held great power over animals. "If you wear this mask and talk to an animal, they may understand."

"Even if you speak English instead of Swahili?" Anna asked.

The carver paused to ponder the question, then nodded his head. "I think there is no problem in how words sound to this rabbit," he said.

Jabari and Anna bargained for the mask. Anna was certain that seventeen thousand shillings, around $40, was a fair price. Jabari motioned her outside the booth and whispered, "We can get it for fifteen thousand shillings, I think."

The carver rose with some difficulty and grasped a thick stick leaning against the post. Anna noticed his right foot was turned out awkwardly. "I think he does interesting work," Anna said. "Let's accept his offer at seventeen thousand."

Jabari glanced at the carver, then back at Anna. He nodded solemnly. "Yes, Mama. You are right."

"What about this one?" She took the little bat-eared fox mask off the post, thinking, at first, that she might buy it for Jabari. The ears were three times the size of the tiny face. "Does it also talk to animals?"

"That one is very small," the carver said. "But I think it has great power over mosquitos."

"So, will it keep malaria away?" Anna asked.

The carver shrugged. "I think it will try," he said. He leaned awkwardly against the post and scratched his leg.

Jabari turned to Anna. "Are you thinking this mask will keep Hami well?"

"I don't know," she said, "but it's worth a try. We can hang it on the post in the garden, and everyone will benefit."

They bargained again and went away with both masks wrapped in newspaper.

§§§

Aaron was working in the hotel room when she returned and unwrapped their new treasures, first the pot. He turned it in his hand and traced the tails of the monkeys. "I like it," he said. "How much did that set us back?"

"About $3.00," Anna said. Then she unwrapped the masks.

He ran his hand over the smooth rabbit ears, the perfectly round eyes, two large teeth behind the wide lips and smiled.

"The carver told us that this mask has power over animals," Anna said. Aaron gave her a look she interpreted as: *when did you lose your mind?*

"I don't suppose there was anything more traditional," he jested, "like maybe a carving of St. Francis?" She ignored him. "Really," she said. "If you wear this mask and speak to the animals, they understand what you are saying."

She took the mask from him and held it up to her face.

194

"I love you, Aaron."

He laughed. "I can't understand a word you're saying."

Then she showed him the little fox mask. "This one has power over mosquitos—maybe. I'm going to hang it on a post on the patio to keep us all well."

He laughed again. "You and Jabari are having way too much fun."

§§§

Aaron and Anna joined the visitors from Transnational Development that evening for dinner. Howard Hammond was ten years older than Aaron, with a commanding presence. Hammond's graying hair, deep-set, dark-brown eyes and full eyebrows made for a strong resemblance to Sean Connery. Like Connery, his eyes smiled first, then his lips turned up slightly.

Nick Icovino, financial vice-president, near retirement and the oldest of the group, sat on Hammond's right. Caleb Weatherly slid into the seat next to Icovino. He was a new employee, a recent Columbia Law School graduate who said he'd grown up in Harlem, and this was his first trip to Africa. "I was always told that my great-great grandfather was taken from Bagamoyo as a slave," he said. "I hope I have a chance to see that town while we're here."

"It was originally spelled Bwagamoyo," Aaron said. "In Swahili, that means something like 'dump out your heart.'"

Caleb nodded. "I understand that there are some heart-wrenching photographs in the museum," he said. "Still, I want to go there because—well, I'm not sure—maybe I just want to connect in some tangible way with my African past."

Carina Sorenstam, in a business-like, below-the-knee black skirt, low heels and a white linen blazer, arrived at the table just as they were ordering. She wore Tiffany signature

"X" silver earrings and a matching pendant on a slim silver chain which settled just below her collarbone. No rings, no bracelets. No hint of Joy perfume. Her hair was darker than Anna remembered, now a medium ash blonde, layered in a short razor cut. She slid into the empty seat on Hammond's left.

Throughout the meal, Anna was drawn to Hammond, anticipating his next Connery smile. She appreciated how he deferred to Aaron when the others posed questions about the country, the mill or the village. She noticed that Carina was wholly focused on Hammond, as if waiting for him to smile at her. Throughout the meal, Carina said very little except to respond to Hammond's remarks with the occasional "you're right" (nodding her head) or "that's true" (twice touching his sleeve).

As they took the last sips of their after-dinner coffee, Howard Hammond said, "I think we've been very productive in our meetings today. Thanks to you, Nick, we've got the numbers we need to win our case. Caleb, you've drawn up an air-tight contract, and Aaron, you've told us exactly what we need to do to make this project succeed. We're ready to meet with the government in the morning. You're a great team."

Anna expected Hammond to say something to Carina next, but he put down his napkin and rose from the table. Carina remained seated, looking quizzically at her boss. It was only when he turned to look down at her that he seemed to realize his omission. "And Carina," he said. "Without you, we would have been floundering in piles of unorganized paperwork. Thank you for keeping us on track."

Anna wondered what Howard Hammond meant, and what Carina's job actually entailed. When the visitors got into the elevator headed for the third floor, she wondered if Carina was booked into a separate room and, if so, if she slept there.

§§§

Anna and Aaron took a walk outside, then wandered through the gift shop. A middle-aged man wearing a business suit, crisp white shirt and blue rep tie approached Aaron and asked them to join him at a table in the lobby. "Mr. Okonjo is an undersecretary at the ministry," Aaron said, introducing him to Anna.

Okonjo removed his blue-tinted glasses. "I look forward to our meeting tomorrow, though it may not be necessary," he said. "I am here tonight to discuss a proposition for you." He told Aaron that the Chief was pleased with his work and would like for him to remain for two more years as general manager, employed directly by the government. To assist him, the government would hire the Indian expatriate that Aaron had recommended as mill manager.

"Of course, you would be on a strict contract and paid the exact salary you now receive, including a month of home leave for you and your wife, completely funded by the government."

Aaron began to chuckle. "Wait, Mr. Chadwick," Okonjo said. "If the mill succeeds in operating and breaks even within one year, you will receive a bonus of two month's salary."

"That is very generous of the Chief," Aaron said, "but I won't leave my company, and I feel our whole team is essential to the success of the project."

He stood up, shook Okonjo's hand and nodded to Anna. Then he turned back to Okonjo. "We'll meet in the morning and, together, we'll fulfill the promise we made to the people of Tanzania."

Okonjo didn't move.

"*Lala visuri*, Mr. Okonjo," Aaron said. "Sleep well. And thank you for your confidence in me."

Aaron was laughing when they got into the elevator. "It's an old trick to retain a manager without paying a management contract," he said. "And us old hands know better than to fall for old tricks."

"Still, I liked the part about the home leave," Anna said.

CHAPTER TWENTY-FOUR: SUCCESS!

*I*n the morning, Jabari took Aaron and the visitors to the ministry and waited for them. Anna's mission was to procure supplies for the after-school program in Ahadi. She walked the downtown streets, looking in every store, but only came away with two plastic kazoos, one set of children's watercolor paints and five exercise books. But, back in the hotel gift shop, she was delighted to find two point-and-shoot Pocket Kodak kits, each including a box of 110 black and white film.

Anna telephoned Christopher from the hotel and awakened him at five in the morning. She asked him to go to Ritz camera store and have them send a dozen of the cheapest point-and-shoot cameras they could find—possibly the Pocket Kodak—plus twenty-four rolls of 110 Tri-X Pan. "Hang the expense. Have them sent DHL," she said. "They're for the school in Ahadi. Use my ATM card and take out some extra. Buy Beryl a nice birthday gift. Maybe some creative earrings from the Vermont State Craft store?"

"We broke up the day after Christmas," he said.

"Oh, Christopher! I'm sorry."

He'd had girlfriends in high school and college, but none seemed serious until Beryl. Anna liked Beryl's sense of humor, her evident appreciation of Christopher and his talents, her down-to-earth manner. She had silky dark brown hair and sparkling brown eyes. Her father was a high school principal, and she was attending Dartmouth on an academic scholarship, working part time at the Dartmouth Book Store.

She appeared genuine compared to several of the other girls he had dated who'd seemed flirtatious or calculating. In fact, Anna had begun to imagine Beryl as a daughter-in-law she could come to love.

"It's okay, Mom. It was my idea, and Beryl's not exactly hurting. I saw her last night at the movies in Hanover with a preppy-type grad assistant."

"I'm still sorry, Christopher. Breakups are never easy."

He didn't respond.

"I miss you, Christopher," she said.

"If it's okay with you, Mom, maybe I could use that ATM card to buy something creative for Darlene?"

"Darlene? That cute girl on the skiing team?"

"No, Darlene, that cute girl who was in my Shakespeare class. She's back here getting her MA."

"Christopher, have you applied yet to any of the grad schools on your list?"

"Who would take care of the house? Who'd feed Murray?"

"We'd work that out, Honey. You come first. Have you even filled out the applications?"

"It's snowing," he said. "I'm going to have to sweep the roof again."

The applications were obviously still in his desk drawer.

"Your dad's shirt cuffs are getting frayed, and I need shoes badly," Anna said.

"I'm not good at buying women's shoes, Mom."

She laughed, remembering the time he bought her too-small pink sandals with sequins and bows for her birthday. He was eleven.

"Along with the cameras, could you throw in a couple of Dad's dress shirts and my white sandals? Your dad's in a big meeting today which could determine how long we'll be here. I'll try to call you again before we leave Dar."

"Okay, Mom. But Murray gets nervous when the phone rings in the middle of the night."

"I love you, Christopher," she said. "We'll talk soon."

"I love you, Mom. Say hi to Dad."

She hung up the phone with a longing to see him coming up the driveway, a camera around his neck, Murray running ahead of him, tugging on a leash. She wanted, in the worst way, to give him a hug.

§§§

Aaron showed up late in the afternoon and summarized what happened at the meeting.

"Hammond pointed out that the Indian takeover bids are too low to cover even a year of interest payments on loans for building the mill. Chief Shasani told Hammond he was right. 'We must practice patience,' Shasani said, 'and create a more valuable investment.'"

Aaron paused and smiled. "We produced our spreadsheet lowering the overall cost of the contract by bringing in all three of the Indian expats I recommended. They come without family, without containers packed with goods, without demands for several months of leave and airfare to the States. We showed how, with some personnel changes, necessary repairs and a few small upgrades—plus a steady supply of electricity and fuel—we could increase productivity and eventually even turn a profit. So, the result is that Transnational Development retains the contract.

"And our good Mr. Shao will be demoted to manager of recreational facilities—which, I believe, currently consists of one tennis court. Of course, that means no office, a lower rank and lower salary, and he will have to vacate his current

201

home and move down to the bottom of the hill without access to a company vehicle. I'm pretty sure his cronies will help him find a more attractive offer somewhere else."

Aaron slipped off his red tie, unbuttoned the top of his shirt and sat on the bed. "While we were still in his office, Chief Shasani called the bank and ordered the manager to cover bills owed for electricity, gas, coal and diesel fuel." He twirled his index finger in the air. "And I have in my briefcase a check which should cover the cost of repairing the generator."

Aaron collapsed onto the bed. "Oh, and if it's okay with you, I stay on as General Manager with the same terms as before, plus a raise this April."

"It's more than okay with me—but for how long?" she asked.

"If all goes well, through March of the following year."

"Okay, but only if we take that trip to the Serengeti you promised me."

"There is nothing I'd rather do. We'll go as soon as the dry season begins. I promise."

"That would be June," she said. "Six months from now."

Aaron shook his head. "Let's see how it goes in the meantime."

"I think it will go very well," Anna said. She remembered her earlier doubts that the project would succeed. How could she have underestimated Aaron? She leaned over to kiss her husband. "You are amazing, Mr. Chadwick."

He returned the kiss and added a longer one before responding. "Mrs. Chadwick, it was a pretty good day. The only downside was that the Chief said there was no available replacement for Dr. Ogbu. We'll have to figure out a way to work around him for a while."

Aaron got up and started to remove his shirt. It was dingy with sweat stains at the neck, and the top of the collar was wearing thin. "You need some new dress shirts," Anna said. "I talked to Christopher."

"I miss the critter," Aaron said.

"Me, too. I wish—" She wished Christopher was still fifteen, or even younger, a child she could still teach and comfort. She wished that he was with them now, though she knew that made no sense. He needed to be independent, building a life that would lead to meaningful work, his own family, to experiences they would no longer share.

"Anna, what did Christopher have to say?"

"He's sending a couple of shirts, but they won't be enough." She paused. "And, I hate to tell you this, but he broke up with Beryl."

"Good. I never liked her all that much."

"Really? I thought she was perfect for Christopher."

"He's too young to be serious about anyone."

"But Aaron, weren't we about the same age when—"

"You were lucky," he said. He grinned. "So was I."

He ran a finger around his shirt collar. "We could stop by the tailor. He could make me a couple of swanky dashikis."

"You would be very fashionable. Maybe with gold embroidery? Beads sewn in?"

He laughed. "You want me to go native?"

Anna dangled her sandals, stained from rain and mud and patched with tape. "Does he also make shoes?"

"I'm sure there are some shredded tires in the auto shop," he said. "We could cut some to fit, and you'd be right in style."

"Thanks, Buddy," she said.

"But you're right. A trip to the Serengeti would do us

both good. I just don't know when I can get away. In the meantime, how would you like to spend tomorrow night in Zanzibar?"

"Really? I'd love it!" Anna said. "But I wish—"

"Yes, I know. Christopher would love to explore Zanzibar."

CHAPTER TWENTY-FIVE: ZANZIBAR

*A*t nine in the morning, Anna and Aaron spotted Howard Hammond and Nick Icovino in line at the breakfast buffet. As Icovino was wearing sunglasses in the restaurant, Anna wondered if he hadn't snuck back down to the bar after dinner the night before.

Hammond put his tray down in a corner booth for four. "What about the others?" Anna asked.

"I think Carina's on a no-breakfast diet," Howard said. He pointed toward Icovino's tray, empty but for two cups of coffee. "It's evidently the latest thing."

"And Caleb?"

"He made a deal with a taxi driver. They were to head off for Bagamoyo at sunrise and would be back at the airport by 4:00 to make Caleb's flight, eventually to Charlotte. A state senator in Raleigh is raising environmental issues about our mill near there, so Caleb's making a stopover before returning home."

Hammond jabbed his fork into a large chunk of pineapple, lifted it toward his mouth then put it back down. "What gets me," he said, "is that particular mill makes nothing but recycled newsprint. There's no pulp being produced, and wastewater is effectively treated through the effluent plant. It's probably one of the cleanest mills in the country. I'm certain Caleb can enlighten the senator."

Hammond raised his fork again and had just bitten into the pineapple when Aaron nudged him. "Look there," Aaron said. Ryder McGowan was grabbing a tray off the buffet.

Hammond swallowed quickly. "That reprehensible son-of-a—" he said.

"That's too kind a description," Anna said, and the men looked at her, surprised. Hammond asked: "What would you call him, Anna?"

"I'm in the company of gentlemen," she said. "Otherwise I'd call him a—" Aaron laughed and put his hand over her mouth. Hammond and Icovino laughed as well.

"I like your wife," Howard Hammond said. "I like forthright women."

"Anna's never been timid," Aaron said.

"—a malicious idiot," she whispered under her breath.

But Anna hadn't really spoken her mind. She pondered why Hammond's possible sexual relationship with an employee was tolerated while McGowan's possible sexual relationship with an employee was reprehensible. Didn't the status of both women make them susceptible to their bosses' advances? The discernable difference, of course, was that Carina Sorenstam, college-educated, a white American, had more options, plus access to birth control pills. Maybe—well, there were a lot of maybes.

"So," said Hammond, "McGowan knocked on my door last night and told me he was ready to go wherever we wanted to send him. I told him we had a job for him in Hell."

"You really said that?" Anna asked.

"Um…not exactly. But I congratulated him on becoming a father and, of course, he denied any intimacy with the girl. He actually blamed Jonas Shao."

"Her name is Layla," Aaron said. "We'll make sure she's taken care of through the delivery. If the baby is mulatto, we'll track down McGowan and hold him responsible. Or try to, at least. If not, well, I have a feeling Shao will be long gone."

"Do all you can," Hammond said. "We have a plane to catch. Keep up the good work, Aaron."

Anna looked closely at the three men as they rose from the table. They were smart, experienced and dedicated to their jobs. A few years ago, no woman would have been traveling with them. It occurred to Anna that, in today's corporate world, both sexes were still learning how to behave under the new gender equality rules, and maybe she'd misunderstood the signals between Howard Hammond and Carina Sorenstam. For Carina's sake, she wanted to believe—was determined to believe unless proven wrong— that the relationship between them was business only, and Carina's contribution to the success of the project was more significant than it appeared.

§§§

Jabari returned from the airport and took Anna and Aaron to the Zanzibar ferry dock. Aaron told him to park the car in a safe place, then pick them up at 5pm the next afternoon.

The sea was rough going over, but the Indian Ocean bright, rich turquoise turning to vibrant blue. They clung to the rails and breathed in briny air that felt lighter, cooler the farther they traveled the some thirty-five nautical miles from Dar Es Salaam. Terns whirled overhead. A school of dolphin steamed by, surfacing and descending into the water, their rhythmic movements mesmerizing. They began to breach, their black bodies sleek, flashes of white underbellies, rising tails. Water steamed from their fins. Anna couldn't take pictures fast enough.

Two hours later they could see the Stone Town dock, and the water turned pure turquoise again. A pair of eagles flew overhead. One plunged into the sea and emerged with a large silver fish gripped in its beak. Anna turned on the Canon motor drive and ran through 10 frames. She hoped one of them produced a printable shot.

They wandered through the slender streets of the ancient city. Anna photographed the intricately-carved wood doors, balconies and window casings, some studded with etched brass, some enhanced by Arabic inscriptions. She photographed the minarets, the spice market, slave market, the shadow of a veiled woman against a stone wall. She followed a little girl guiding a wobbly hoop around a narrow corner. In a light rain, a portent of the season approaching, she stood sheltered in a doorway to take half a dozen pictures of the child. *Click. Click. Click.* It was, to Anna, as if Stone Town were created just to be filmed.

After the skies cleared in the late afternoon, Aaron ambled off on his own to the boatyard. Anna found a row of market stalls and bought him a dashiki—cotton printed yellow with broad blue stripes and waves of green across the bottom and up the sleeves, a yoke of blue flowers which looked more like pitchforks than flowers. He eyed it with puzzlement but wore it to dinner at the hotel. When they returned to the room, he looked at himself in the mirror. "Hmmm," he said. "How do you think this will look with my blue blazer and the Kandinsky tie you bought me in London?"

Anna smiled. "Not bad, but it might be a little hard to tuck under a leather belt."

§§§

In the morning they hired a taxi to tour the main island. The driver pulled up to a long expanse of white sand beach, the Indian Ocean beyond a brilliant turquoise. Strands of cirrus clouds floated lazily above the calm sea. They asked the driver to wait, took off their shoes and headed down the beach, their footprints following them in the sand.

A light breeze blew off the water, and gentle waves lapped the shore, receded and returned in a tranquil, hypnotic rhythm. "Imagine," Anna said, "this sea has been ebbing and flowing since it was formed, way before human beings were created, and never once contained the exact same molecules of water, never touched the coast in exactly the same way."

As she stood there, contemplating a sea that stretched all the way to Sumatra, circled Australia, became the Coral Sea, the Tasman Sea, the Pacific Ocean, Anna realized that there were many villages like Ahadi across the globe, and no place that lacked for pain.

She considered how the passage of time meant changes, and wondered what changes, in years to come, might relieve the suffering she saw day after day in Ahadi, the suffering she felt so powerless to ease.

Yet, despite the pain, there was also joy. She surmised that, in years to come, she would find herself longing for another day in Ahadi—filling a market basket with peanuts and soap powder, working with Hami in the garden, urging children to embrace possibility, watching a mysterious man with a spear disappear through the bushes. She imagined dark nights in the future when she would yearn for Ahadi's breathtaking array of stars.

She photographed Aaron gazing out toward the horizon, then took his hand, and they stood together at the shoreline, water swirling around their bare feet.

"I think I'll always remember this moment," Anna said, "this moment of nothing appearing to happen, yet everything about it feeling significant."

A Tanzanian Story

CHAPTER TWENTY-SIX: JOSEPH

*B*y the first of March, the rainy season was underway. Anna wasn't even aware that the new Indian expatriates had arrived until she passed the four of them piled into a Suzuki and headed for the market down the hill. None brought family; all seemed to spend long days working at the mill and quiet evenings at home. Aaron reported that the rest of the managers were happily going about the business of making paper and administering various aspects of the mill, township and the woodlands.

Anna and Eva continued to work in the darkroom once or twice a week. They were developing a roll of black and white pictures from Zanzibar, when Eva said, "I have never seen that kind of water."

"That's the Indian Ocean," Anna said. "Have you never been to Dar?

"No, Mama. It is too far away."

"Have you ever seen a *tembo*?"

She shook her head.

"A *twiga*?"

"I have seen your pictures of *twigas*." She stretched her neck. "I think they are very tall—and strange."

"Next time we go to Dar, perhaps you should go with us. You can see the ocean and, maybe, on the way, you can see a *tembo* and a *twiga*."

Her eyes fairly danced with excitement. "Oh, Mama, is that possible?"

"I think so," Anna said. "But, before that happens, I

wonder if you would help me teach the children photography in the after-school program."

Eva turned serious. "I don't know enough," she said.

"You can translate for me. And help me print their photographs."

"I can do that, Mama."

On Tuesday afternoon, they walked down to the school where excited children were gathering in the muddy courtyard. Grace Kapera read from a sheet of paper to call out the names of the clubs and the rooms where each one would meet. The children raced to their assigned places, laughing, clapping, clasping the hands of friends. Twelve children, five boys and seven girls from age seven to thirteen, had signed up for the photography club.

Anna asked Eva to tell the children that they would be assigned photographs to take, and the best would be developed for them to keep. Today they would learn how a camera works.

She divided them into two groups and gave the oldest child in each group one of the two Kodaks she'd bought in Dar. Then she described the parts of the camera. The children seemed interested but unsure of themselves. Next, she passed out photographs she'd taken. They laughed over the picture of the giraffe's head twisted around the palm tree. "*Twiga, twiga,*" they whispered to each other. "Oh, Maasai," they said with a degree of awe, staring at the picture of the two young herders and their spears. When they saw the photograph of Grace Kampera, they all but shouted, "*Mwalimu mkuu.*"

"They like their head teacher," Eva said.

"I like her, too," Anna said.

She asked the children to comment on why the pictures

appealed to them. A small boy raised his hand then rose from his seat. "I can see the eyelashes on the *twiga*," he said

"So the head is in focus," Anna said. "But what about the mountains behind the *twiga*?"

"Maybe they are far away?" an older girl said.

"The camera is focused on the *twiga* head," Anna said. "So it is clear, but the mountains in the distance would distract from the subject—the *twiga*—so they are are meant to be fuzzy."

"What about the two Maasai?" she continued. "What do you want the camera to see?"

One by one, the children raised their hands and stood to speak: "The spears," "the beads," "the faces," "the eyes." The children were animated and seemed to be enjoying the lesson. But Anna didn't want to test their patience. She decided to wait for a later session before addressing lighting and cropping. She directed them to go outside.

"Eva," she said, "tell them to pair off with a partner." The children formed groups of two. "Now, I want you to tell each other what you like best to do." Eva translated and the children whispered to each other. "Each of you will take a picture of your camera partner," Anna said. "But your partner must be pretending to do what they most like to do."

One older girl was lying down, as if asleep; another was squatting, pretending to eat, while one of the youngest danced and another pretended to read. Joseph, a slight boy with a prominent forehead, elfin chin, large brown eyes and dimpled smile, pretended to throw a spear. His camera partner, Ashur, whirled around, arms outstretched like a bird. Another small boy ran over to a girl and kissed her. All the children laughed. Eva told the ones being photographed to hold still, and she and Anna helped those taking the pictures

213

to frame the shots and push the button.

They had just finished up when the other children began to emerge from the adjacent classrooms, running, smiling. One group, the music club, came out singing, swaying to a Swahili song. Another group, the English Club, was also singing, their voices boisterous with excitement: "John Jacob Jingleheimer Schmidt. His name is my name too..."

Children from the cooking club came next, still chewing the pancakes Tobias had taught them to make. It looked to Anna as if the afterschool activities were going to be a great success.

At the end of the week, Anna inspected the negatives of the pictures the children had taken. Some were a little blurry; some not quite centered, with a foot or part of a head missing, but all were printable. And, over the weekend, with a little darkroom magic, all would, hopefully, become treasures for the children.

§§§

It was raining heavily when Anna and Eva entered the classroom the next Tuesday. The children were sitting silently on their benches. "Your pictures!" Anna said. "*Nzuri*. Very good."

The children looked up, expectantly, but showed none of their usual excitement. Anna began to hand out the prints: the dancing girl, the reading girl, the kissing boy. Each child looked carefully at the picture and smiled, but there were no giggles. Anna wondered, at first, if the dreary weather were to blame. No, something else was amiss.

She held up the picture of the boy pretending to throw a spear. "Joseph, *ndiyo*?" The children nodded and turned their faces away. Anna scanned the room. The boy was not there.

She handed Ashur the picture Joseph had taken of him pretending to fly. It was by far the best picture—taken from a low angle so that Ashur's head looked up into the sky and his arms spread at a slant across the horizon. Ashur took the picture in both hands, smiled and held it to his chest.

Anna whispered to Eva. "We have a problem. Can you ask them what they know about Joseph?" The first thought that occurred to Anna was that Joseph was sick. But he'd been healthy the week before—animated, bright, eyes alert and flashing with fun. Then she wondered if a parent might have removed Joseph from the photography group fearing that taking his photograph would capture his soul. She had heard that there were still animists in the village who believed that representational images—pictures, mirrors, voodoo dolls—could steal souls. She had learned that a witch doctor could retrieve a soul, but perhaps the juju would fail, and the person whose soul was stolen would go through life pitied or, even worse, outcast, believing there was no purpose to their existence.

Anna handed out the remaining photographs and waited nervously as Eva walked down the aisle and sat down beside the two oldest girls in the middle of the room. Ashur and another boy sitting on the bench in front of them turned to listen. Eva nodded, finally rose, walked back up the aisle and pulled Anna aside.

"Joseph is Dr. Ogbu's son," she said. "Ogbu said boys should be playing sports, not taking pictures like girls. But Joseph wanted to be in this club. Besides, he is somewhat small for football and has no interest in track. There were not enough tennis racquets available, so there will be no tennis. Joseph hasn't been at school for three days now."

Anna nodded. She'd try to find Joseph and make sure

he was okay. She'd enlist Grace Kampera's support to make sure the boy returned to school. If necessary, she'd ask Aaron to speak to Dr. Ogbu. She would do all she could to bring Joseph back. But, right now, she had to regain the interest of the students in the room. She reached into the basket beside her and brought out the Kodak Pocket cameras sent from Vermont, each labelled with a child's name.

"Okay," she said, and Eva translated. "Now, we have a camera for each of you—and we will make sure Joseph gets one, too." Each child looked at her, unblinking, as if to be assured they were being told the truth. The two older girls jumped up and danced in place.

"The cameras are yours to use during the club meetings. You must return them at the end of each day. You will have one roll of film now to take 24 pictures in the next three weeks. We will take small walks to photograph special places. If you take too many pictures today or next week, you won't be able to take any more. When the roll is finished, Eva or I will help you rewind the film. Understand?"

"At the end of that time," she said, "you will come in small groups to my home to learn how to make pictures from your film."

Some of the children giggled; some shook their heads. The two smallest ones, a girl and a boy at the front of the room, looked at each other with questioning eyes, then eyed her suspiciously. She knelt down in front of them. "Yes. *Ndiyo.*" She pointed at one, then the other. *Wewe pia.* You, too." Slow grins began to emerge on their faces.

She passed out the cameras. The children looked closely at them, turned them over, pushed buttons, held them up to their eyes. "Now, Eva, let's teach them how to load film into the cameras."

§§§

The rain had stopped by the time the group was dismissed. Anna went to the office to talk to Grace Kampera, but she wasn't in, so she left a note to contact her on an urgent matter. Anna wanted, in the worst way, to confront the doctor, change his mind, embrace Joseph and tell him how special he was. She knew that was the wrong approach.

As they walked up the muddy hill, Anna said to Eva: "I want to talk to Doctor Ogbu, but I know it's not my place. Even if I found him, I don't think I would be able to convince him to allow Joseph to come back to school. Perhaps Grace will know what to tell him."

Nevertheless, Anna asked Eva if she knew where Dr. Ogbu lived. "It is near here, the third house on the very next street," Eva said.

They turned the corner into Kwanza Street. Anna looked at the row of houses, their small, muddy yards, a few well-tended flowering bushes. So many families had brought relatives with them when they moved to Ahadi, and it was easy to understand why. While no acres of farmland adjoined the houses, there were amenities not available in most villages—electric cookers, fans, tap water.

"Which house?" Anna asked.

"That one, with the Land Cruiser parked in the driveway," Eva said.

As they stood looking down Kwanza Street, Eva said, "I have an idea. If you wait here, I will go knock on the back door and try to talk to Elena, the house girl. She is my cousin's friend. She will tell me about Joseph."

Anna agreed. "Take the picture Ashur made of him," she said. "In fact, take his camera, too." She rummaged through the basket she was carrying and retrieved the camera assigned

217

to him. "If Joseph is there, Elena can give it to him. But tell her he has to return to school to get the film."

Anna paced the corner of the street until Eva returned, no longer carrying the camera and grinning. "I saw Joseph standing just outside the kitchen, listening. And, as the door was closing, he was running toward Elena to get the picture and the camera."

"Wonderful!" Anna said. "I think we will see him next week."

Eva turned off the road to walk the dirt path to her parents' house outside the village, and Anna continued up the hill. Just as she arrived home, Grace Kampera pulled up on her scooter. "I have been making inquiries," Grace said, "as to why Joseph was missing school. I learned that his father told the football coach there will be no medicine for his family or members of the team if Joseph is not allowed to play. The coach, naturally, said Joseph was welcome."

Grace leaned the scooter on the kickstand. "They had a special practice Saturday afternoon," she continued, "and Dr. Ogbu brought his son. But as soon as his father left, the bigger boys began to tease Joseph about being small and about his daddy driving him around in a big car. One shoved a ball into his face. The coach stopped the practice and told the boys there would be no more games if they couldn't play as a team. I only learned this late yesterday."

"Was the team disbanded?" Anna asked.

Grace shook her head. "No. They played this afternoon."

"And Joseph, did he play?"

"No. When he didn't come to school this morning, I went to the house. The car was in the driveway, but nobody came to the door. As I turned the corner to return to school, Dr. Ogbu sped past me in the Land Cruiser. He didn't look in my direction. I waited until he was out of sight and returned to the house. Mrs. Ogbu was in the courtyard. As soon as she saw me, she slipped inside the door. I think she only speaks a tribal dialect common in Nsukka, Nigeria, where she and Dr. Ogbu lived before he came to Tanzania."

"How does she survive here without speaking Kiswahili or English?" Anna asked.

"She is not often here," Grace replied. "She returns to Nigeria for months at a time."

"Does she not take Joseph?"

"No, Joseph is the son of Mama Joseph, Dr. Ogbu's second wife, a Tanzanian." She shook her head. "While it is customary for all wives and children to live together in the household, Mama Joseph is usually at the Doctor's home in Dar Es Salaam when his Nigerian wife is here in Ahadi. She takes the little ones, girls three and five, with her. We assume one of the reasons this Mrs. Ogbu spends so much time in Nigeria is that there are other children there, as well."

"Whoa!" Anna exclaimed. "So Joseph is living in the house with his father who insists that he play soccer—I mean football—and his mother and little sisters are in Dar Es Salaam, while another woman, not his mother—a woman with whom he cannot communicate—is sleeping with his father? And she probably has children she leaves in West Africa when visiting her husband here?"

Grace nodded, her eyes troubled. "It is true."

"No wonder Joseph wants to learn to express himself with a camera," Anna said. "Did you see him at the house?"

"No. I now think maybe Dr. Ogbu has sent him off to his mother in Dar or enrolled him in a private boarding school somewhere."

"No. Joseph is home," Anna said, and told her of Eva's

conversation with the house girl.

Grace sighed. "There is a law that a child must attend school," she said. "I'll have the personnel manager, Emmanuel Chiza, talk to Dr. Ogbu. Chiza is president of the schoolboard. If that doesn't work, I'll go to security. This Dr. Ogbu causes too much trouble."

She rubbed her hand against her forehead and closed her eyes. "I will never forget how he was responsible for my sister—for the baby—my nephew—who never lived."

Anna put her arm around Grace's shoulder. She wanted to tell her that Aaron had tried to have the doctor fired, but the Chief had said there was no replacement. Though she trusted Grace completely, she knew she couldn't impart that kind of information to anyone in the village, so she simply said: "If necessary, I know Aaron will be eager to help."

§§§

Grace was walking her scooter out of the driveway when Aaron pulled up in the Suzuki. Anna met him at the car and told him about Joseph. "That poor kid," he said. "If Grace Kampera or Emanuel Chiza need my assistance, I am more than happy to step in."

As he and Anna entered the house, Aaron filled her in on the latest news about Jonas Shao. "I called him into the office this morning and told him about his new assignment as recreation facilities manager. He argued that he was too well educated and too valuable to the company to have such a demeaning job. We discussed his negative value to the company and the Chief's decision. Shao threatened to have me deported. I laughed, and he backed out of my office and fled."

Once inside the house, Aaron dropped his briefcase beside the door and continued the story. "Evidently Shao raced home, instructed his wife, teen-age daughter and cook to pack up all they could and left Ahadi ten minutes later in his company Land Cruiser."

"But that's—"

"You're right," Aaron said. "That's thievery. So I sent the chief security officer after him. The folks waiting for a ride at the gate said he was racing toward Mbeya. The officer found the car outside a motel at the edge of Mbeya and went to the police station. By the time they returned to the motel, the vehicle and the Shaos were gone. That means there is one less Land Cruiser in Ahadi, and ours is, of course, in the shop with a busted headlight."

A Tanzanian Story

CHAPTER TWENTY-SEVEN: LAYLA

*T*he next morning, Aaron was just getting into the Suzuki to go to work when Ryder McGowan's former house girl, Layla, appeared, again wearing her violet *kanga*. Draped over her shoulders was another *kanga*, dark blue, bordered with large yellow sunflowers. Her feet were bare.

Anna stepped outside. Layla looked at her rather than Aaron. "The nurse has said I should go to Iringa because the baby may be hard to be born."

She rubbed her full stomach and shifted her stance from one foot to the other. "I would have asked my father to take me, but he is ashamed and doesn't speak to me now."

"Layla," Aaron said. "I don't know your father. Does he have access to one of our vehicles?"

"He is not here," she said, looking into the distance. "He works at the tea plantation in Mufindi." She winced, shifted her weight again and grasped her belly in her hands. "I also tried to ask Mr. Shao if he would take me, but he is somehow gone away."

Anna remember that Ryder McGowan had blamed the pregnancy on Shao. "How do you know Jonas Shao?" she asked. Layla looked down at her bare toes, tinged orange from wet clay. "He used to visit us—Mr. McGowan," she said. "Since he has a car and a driver, I thought Mr. Shao might—."

"Layla," Aaron said, "Doctor Ogbu has been seeing you regularly as I directed. Is that not right?"

She nodded. "Only one time. Since then he is too busy."

"But you saw the nurse today?"

She shook her head. "Two days ago. She told me to go to the hospital in Iringa. Since then I have been trying to find a way."

"I told you to come to me if you needed help," Aaron said.

"Baba GM, I am sorry. I didn't want to bring you my trouble." Her eyes were moist. She winced again.

"We'll get you there," he said. "The Suzuki is not a good choice as the ride is too bumpy."

Tears trickled down both her cheeks.

"Do you have what you need to go and stay in the hospital for a few days?"

She nodded and opened her wrap and showed them a small yellow string bag tied above her extended belly.

"Come inside and sit down," Aaron said.

Anna put her arm around Layla and led her to the loveseat. Aaron went to the desk, pulled a piece of paper from his wallet, lifted the phone, checked the paper and dialed a number.

"*Jambo.* This is the GM. Why are you not at work?" He scowled while listening. "Yes. Yes. I don't care. I expect you in your office immediately and your driver and Land Cruiser at my home within five minutes."

He paused, looked at the ceiling and waved his index finger in the air. "It's an emergency. Five minutes or—"

Again, he listened, now pumping his fist in anger. "I'll tell you later, and you'll get your car back by morning. If you value your job, your Land Cruiser will be here in five minutes."

He shook his head while listening. "Yes. I meant what I

said. *Right now.* And while we're at it, make sure your son is in school today." He slammed down the phone and checked his watch.

"Aaron, I want to go to Iringa with Layla," Anna said.

"That's good of you," he said, "but I want to try something else first."

He flipped through the pamphlet of phone listings sitting on the desk and dialed another number. "*Jambo.* This is the GM. Who's working today?" He waited for the answer. "Okay. Good. Put Rebecca on." He nodded at Layla. "We'll get you there," he said.

Finally, he spoke into the phone. "I want you to go to Iringa with a patient. In ten minutes. You may have to spend the night." He listened. "Right. *Dakika kumi.* Ten minutes. *Asante sana.*"

Eight minutes later Doctor Ogbu's car arrived. The driver, Daniel, opened the back door and Layla eased her way in. Aaron told Daniel to stop by the clinic on the way out. "The nurse, Rebecca, will be waiting for you," he said.

When the car took off, Anna turned to Aaron. "Dr. Ogbu was evidently not at the clinic. How did you know where to reach him?" she asked.

He smiled. "I was able, by devious means, to procure his private, unlisted home number. If he hadn't answered, I would have tried the Bwana club."

§§§

Several days later Jabari and Anna made a run to Iringa in the repaired Land Cruiser. Before returning home, they stopped at the hospital to check on Layla. Jabari flinched as they walked through the door, but stopped, took a deep breath and walked to the signboard to find directions to the postnatal ward. Layla's baby boy had been delivered by Cesarean section.

They spoke to the doctor who said she was ready to be released, but only if she could return to Ahadi with them in the car.

Jabari pulled up to the entrance; Layla got into the back seat and kept the child hidden behind her *kanga* until he began to wail. When she unfolded the wrap and reached down to soothe his forehead, Anna looked in the rearview mirror and saw him for the first time. His eyes were black and his skin dark brown. Maybe Ryder McGowan was off the hook. But maybe not entirely.

§§§

Layla directed them down a dirt road eight kilometers from Ahadi and told Jabari to stop beside a small house with wattle and daub walls and a straw roof. A tall woman peered out from a faded blue curtain which served as the door. While securing her *kanga* around her waist, she ran toward the car. Layla handed her the baby. He began to cry when the woman took him in her arms. She rocked him and cooed. Layla sighed heavily, stepped slowly from the car and followed the woman carrying the still-crying child through the curtained door.

"Who is that, Jabari? Do you know?"

"I am not certain, Mama," he said. "But I have seen her arrive at the market a few times in Dr. Ogbu's car."

Anna could only guess that she was one of Ogbu's mistresses, a woman with a generous heart who understood the girl's predicament and offered to take her in. She wondered how it would be for Layla, entering the cold, unlit house of a near stranger. She imagined Layla strapping the child to her back the next morning, carrying a clay pot on her head, struggling down the hill to the stream to wash cloth diapers, to fill the pot with water. Her heart ached for the girl.

As they passed through the gate to enter Ahadi, Anna

noticed in the light from the headlamps a figure turning from the road into a path through a stand of eucalyptus trees. As they approached the path, the lights glinted off a raised spear and a loincloth, bright white against his dark skin.

§§§

When they reached home, the front porch light was on, and a man wearing a tan business suit and bright red beret was standing beside a late-model black Audi parked in the drive. As Aaron stepped out from the front door, the man put his hands together and bowed slightly.

Jabari and Anna gathered the groceries from the boot. Jabari took a load around to the back door, but Anna stopped to listen. "Mr. Chadwick," the man said and flashed a sly smile at Aaron, "I have chosen you."

"Ah, I believe I saw you in Mr. Shao's office just before Christmas," Aaron replied.

"Mr. Shao, yes, there is no finer director of finance in all East Africa. He directed me to see you personally." The man handed Aaron a business card and repeated himself: "I have chosen you, Mr. Chadwick."

"East African Supply Company headquartered in Njombe. I recognize this card," Aaron said. "And as I recall, just before I came to the mill, your shipment of sulphuric acid was short by a third of the amount ordered."

Aaron paused, and the man shook his head. "Also, at the same time, your invoice for a large shipment of sodium salts was paid, though no salts were delivered."

"Oh," said the man, appearing surprised. "How can that be? Our accounting system is most accurate."

"And," Aaron added, "your current bid for chemicals is the highest of all those tendered."

The man removed his beret and held it in his hand. "Our

bid is high? That is not possible." Then he looked up at Aaron, and his smile brightened. "Mr. Chadwick, I am sure you realize that our products are much superior to others."

Aaron shook his head in bemusement. "Mr—." He looked at the business card. "Mr. Mnyani, excuse me now. My wife has just arrived from Iringa, and—"

Mnyani glanced behind him at Anna, still standing by the car, nodded quickly and turned back to Aaron. "But, Mr. Chadwick, of all the people I might have chosen to receive our fine products, I have chosen you."

Aaron laughed. "I am honored, my friend." He reached out to shake Mnyani's hand, and Mnyani grabbed it in both of his hands. "*Kwaheri,*" Aaron said, stepping backwards and releasing the grip. "*Safari Njema.*" He walked over to Anna, gave her a peck on the cheek and took the bag of groceries from her hands.

After they entered the house, Anna peeked out the front window. The Audi was still in the driveway. Aaron dropped the groceries in the kitchen and stood next to her. "He was just doing his job—as best as he knows how. But I think we now have a lead on finding Jonas Shao and our stolen Land Cruiser."

§§§

Two days later Aaron came home bringing outdated copies of the *International Herald-Tribune* and the latest local news. A policeman had arrived at the mill to report that Shao was in jail in Njombe, and his Land Cruiser could be retrieved there.

After dinner, Anna sat down to read the papers Aaron had brought. The IRA had launched a mortar attack on #10 Downing Street. In a later edition, Anna read that they exploded bombs at London's Paddington and Victoria stations. Here, in Ahadi, while there were plenty of distasteful shenanigans, there still appeared to be tolerance, even acceptance, between Muslims and Christians and Hindus.

Even Hami had finally received his father's blessing to marry Eva.

A Tanzanian Story

CHAPTER TWENTY-EIGHT: A WEDDING

*R*amadan began the third full week in March. Eva confided to Anna that she had converted to Islam. Her parents had met with Hami's parents and settled on the bride price. She requested permission to iron clothes from noon to 1:30 so she could close the door to the bedroom and pray as she worked instead of thinking about eating.

Hami disappeared from the garden for an hour each noon and seemed to show the effects of fasting when he sat down with Anna for a Wednesday afternoon lesson. Or so Anna thought. He was definitely distracted.

"What are you thinking about, Hami?"

"I am thinking Shawwal is just next month, and that is the time for marrying. There is much to do before then."

Anna handed him a notebook and asked him to use the past tense to write some paragraphs about getting married. While Anna went to the kitchen to check on Tobias' progress with canning tomatoes, Hami bent over the page and began to write:

"One day I was working in the GM garden when Eva first came to work also. She was then sixteen. I greeted her and she replied well, and I was very pleaseed to talk to her. My question asked her as follows: 'Have you got married, or no because I liked to talk about marriage. She said yes she could. Our discussion ended in agreement. I told my parents to propose about that girl whom I liked to marry, but they were not happy to hear that news because this

girl was baptise. My father he said he should find another girl but I ~~cannot~~ not liked to marry other.

Then Eva, she return^ed to work and said she pure still and I was happy because she decided to read Koran and said the shahada, no God but Allah and Mohammed messenger of Allah ~~to become~~ and became like me Muslim. And my father he then ~~say~~ said okay. My parents and her parents they set all together to rearrange dowry and they agreement was successfully to me. The dowry was four cows and gots, but we had not cows or gots, only chickens, so instead it costed fifty shillings thousand and five hundred that my father supposed to pay. I then ~~spended~~ spent marry time to buy metal pot, spoons and kitenges for her."

Anna returned and read the paragraphs, praising Hami for his use of the past tense. She decided to tackle the mistakes in another lesson. "Eva told me that the dowry had been settled. I am so happy for you, Hami. When will you marry?"

"Shawwal follows Ramadan, Mama. And it is Islam tradition to marry on a Sunday during Shawwal. My aunt says it is because that is when the camel has a baby inside."

Anna smiled. It seemed fitting that weddings should occur during the gestation period for camels, as it signified a new generation of animals essential to desert regions.

"It is coming soon, Mama," Hami said. "Eva's mother has even agreed to choose her friend, Bahari Laruu, to be the Sumo to Eva. Mama Laruu some time ago married into our faith."

"What is the Sumo?" Anna asked.

"She will stay with Eva before the marriage and make

her smooth and beautiful and prepare her for the bed." He hesitated, then smiled. "I think Eva is already beautiful."

"I agree," Anna said. "Where will you and Eva have the ceremony?"

Hami shifted in his seat and ran his hand down the spiral of the notebook. "In our family tradition, the papers are signed by the parents and man to be married. The bride girl does not attend the signing. She stays hidden until the man goes to her. My father and uncle did not ever see their wives until that very moment."

"Were they disappointed?"

Hami laughed. "They were lucky. Both my mother and my aunt are pretty. My oldest brother—well, hmm."

"He was not so lucky?"

"He now has two wives. The second one he chose for himself."

"Will you have another wife in time, Hami?"

He shook his head vigorously. "No, Mama. I learned from my brother that one is enough. Besides, I cannot love anyone as much as I love Eva."

"That is very good," Anna said. Even back in the days when she pondered Aaron's faithfulness, when she occasionally flirted with another man, she couldn't imagine loving anyone as much as she did Aaron.

"Where will the papers be signed? And will you have a party following?"

"My uncle wants the ceremony at his house. And he says he can only afford for forty guests to come to the signing and happy time afterwards."

"And Eva?"

Hami shook his head. "She will not be there. It is not the way of my people."

"Where will you live?"

Hami looked at Anna in consternation. "I must now move from my uncle's house because my room there is one of the outside servant rooms. It is very small. If I still lived in my village, even now I be building a house on my father's land. But in Ahadi, I must be big shot inside the mill to have a house."

He shrugged his shoulders and looked out over the garden, the flowers a splendid array of shapes and colors. His eyes showed excitement, then concern.

Anna started to ask him if he would like a job at the mill but realized neither he nor Eva had the skills to warrant them even the smallest company house. Besides, to try to get either of them a position at the mill would be the kind of favoritism she and Aaron were trying to discourage.

Hami continued, "Tobias has said we can build shelter on his land until we can buy. I am even now gathering poles."

Anna smiled at Tobias' generosity, for the shelter would surely consume some part of his vegetable garden.

§§§

Two weeks before the wedding, Anna noticed Hami standing just inside the canopy covering the patio, rain streaming down behind him. He shifted from foot to foot, then looked up as Anna opened the door. "Mama," he said, "my uncle invites you and the GM to come to the wedding." He thrust an envelope into her hand and regarded her with a hopeful expression.

Anna took the envelope and told Hami that she and the GM would be honored to come. He smiled, bowed slightly and ran off in the rain toward the tool shed.

Anna opened the envelope to a white vellum invitation.

Familia ya
shangazi/mjomba
Mahibu Kamala
Ahadi
Wana furaha ya kukaribisha:
Mama & Baba GM
Juu ya harusi ya mpwa wao mpendwa
Hami
kwa
Eva
Kufanyika katika
109 mtaa wa kupendeza
4/18/1991
Saa 4:00 jioni
Na baadaye baada ya kufanyika katika sikukuu

Majibu (Kwa wasiofika tu)
Mahibu Kamala
Simu 25746 Ahadi

"Uh, Hami!" she called out to him. "I think I need a little help here."

Hami ran back, grinning, shook the rain from his head and provided her with a translation.

"It says, Mama, that the family of Aunt/Uncle Mahib Kamala of Ahadi, they are happy to invite you, Mama & Baba GM, on the wedding of their beloved nephew—that's me, Hami—to Eva, done in 109 Pleasant Street, Sunday, April 18, 1991 at 4:00. And later the after-done feast.'"

"And what's the bottom part?" she asked.

"That is how to answer the invitation by calling his very phone number."

Anna laughed. "I will call as soon as the rain ends if the phone is then working."

He looked up at the dark sky. "Oh, no, Mama, that will

be a long time from now. Maybe too late!"

"I will give you a note of acceptance which you can take to your uncle this afternoon. Will that be okay?"

"Yes, Mama. I am honored that you and the GM will be there."

Two days later, a Suzuki pulled up to the door, and a woman whom Anna had never seen before handed her a thin kraft-paper envelope addressed to Mr. & Mrs. GM. Without speaking, the woman ran back to the car and sped away. Inside the envelope was a scrap of thin paper with a brief note, typewritten and photocopied in English. The blanks were filled in by hand.

> To: Prof/Dr/Mr/Mrs/Miss GM .
> The family is glad to
> inform you of the wedding
> preparations for Hami Kamala to
> Eva Pengo due to take place April
> 18 in Ahadi. For the
> success of the occasion, the
> preparation committee kindly
> request your financial
> assistance. Minimum 20,000/= .
> Please submit donation before
> April 1 to Bahari Laruu.
> Thanking you in advance,
> The Preparation Committee

Anna assumed that the amount of shillings requested was adjusted for each recipient, based on what the preparation committee felt they could or should contribute. Still, the request for nearly $50 seemed excessive for food and decorations for a ceremony Eva would not be able to attend. She knew she and Aaron would contribute what was asked, but she would have preferred to give the money to the two of them toward purchase of something of value—such as land on which to build a home.

§§§

The wedding in the small back yard behind Hami's aunt and uncle's house was launched in a downpour at exactly 4:00pm. All the guests—men clustered on the left and women on the right—were huddled under hand-held umbrellas. Bunches of large paper flowers, strung high across the yard and wrapped around the banana trees, dribbled pink and yellow and lavender dye upon the umbrellas. Lanterns flickered around the edge of the yard. In the middle of the small roofed patio, a card table was covered with a white cloth strewn with pink rose petals.

When Anna and Aaron arrived, Hami was standing at the card table with three other men, each with pens ready to sign the marriage documents. Anna recognized Hami's uncle, and assumed the other men were Eva's and Hami's fathers.

The women—family members in matching pink frilly dresses and others in brightly-colored *kangas*—burst into broad smiles and high-pitched cries of "u-lu-lu-lu-lu" after each signature was added to the document and, again, after each of the seven speeches, and, once more, upon the arrival of food and soft drinks which were set up on folding tables.

Anna stood at the edge of the covered patio to watch. She wished she had thought to ask if she could take pictures as she knew she would have felt more comfortable had she been moving through the crowd, half-hidden by her camera.

After the rain tapered off to an intermittent drizzle, three musicians appeared. One beat a goat-skin drum, one brandished a set of rattles and one plucked a zeze, which seemed to have been formed by stringing two bicycle wires from the bottom of a hollowed-out gourd to the top of a long, carved stick.

The musicians settled into a corner of the yard and began to play at an enthusiastic tempo. The women danced, swinging arms and hips with joyous abandon. The end of the song was hailed by a chorus of "u-lu-lu-lu-lu." Then the women began to sing as they danced, still ending the next song with "u-lu-lu-lu-lu" and, by the third song, a few of the men were also singing, then dancing, though still separated from the women by a strict if invisible barrier.

All the while, Hami stood to the side and looked somber. He wore a black suit, the cuffs an inch above his shirtsleeves, the red tie Aaron had loaned him, and a red rose sagging from the right lapel. The only time he smiled was when Aaron, relegated to the men's side, spoke to him, obviously making a joke.

When Hami's aunt walked over to the patio to welcome her, Anna asked: "Why does Hami look so sad?"

"It is the custom," his aunt said. "Marriage is serious."

"Indeed, it is," Anna said. But she remembered how joyous she felt on her wedding day. She was dismayed that Eva couldn't participate in this exuberant ceremony and reception. But then, again, perhaps Eva would have been required to appear as solemn as Hami did.

Anna also wondered why there were no children attending the celebration. Then, from the corner of her eye, she saw two young girls, around seven years old, wearing small versions of the frilly pink dress. They peeked around the house, entered the yard and began to toss rose petals from small raffia baskets, then ran to the back gate. The members of the band jumped up to follow them. First Hami, then his father and uncle, then a few of the other men and most of the women joined the procession. Anna assumed that the children were leading the guests to Eva's house.

As much as Anna wanted to see Eva scrubbed and powdered, perhaps hennaed, surely coiffed and dressed to perfection, lying in wait on a bed covered in fragrant flower petals, she knew if she joined the procession, she would feel like an intruder. She was certain Aaron would feel the same way. She signaled to him across the yard and slipped out to the right of the house. He met her out front. It began to rain again, and he popped open his umbrella.

"The preparation committee certainly put our donation to good use," he said. "Music, dancing, garden décor and just the right amount of—" He looked around to make sure they were alone, laughed, then, in falsetto, sang "u-lu-lu-lu-luu-uuuu."

"U-lu-lu-lu-lu-luuu-uuu," Anna sang back. "I've never seen such sheer joy. Do you suppose the dour native New Englanders could take up ululation?"

A Tanzanian Story

PART FOUR

Tubariki Watoto wa Africa
Bless Us, Children of Africa

May through July, 1991

CHAPTER TWENTY-NINE: CHICKENSHIT

*I*n early May, the rains began to subside. The mid-morning sun was bright when Anna opened the front door to go to the market. On the outside knob, swaying from a length of string, a cascade of white feathers hung from two bony orange chicken feet. Blood dripped onto the front step from the neck where the bird had been decapitated.

Anna dropped her market basket beside the door and looked up and down the street, but nobody was in sight. She raced to the desk and lifted the phone to call Aaron. There was no dial tone. Hami and Tobias were in the garden. Eva was cleaning the back bathroom. As much as Anna wanted to ask one of them to help her remove the bird, she didn't want to alarm them. She ran to the kitchen for a pair of scissors and a garbage bag, then returned to the front door. She averted her eyes while she held the bag under the bird and snipped the string.

Anna tied the bag tightly and threw it into the outside trash bin, then grabbed her basket and hurried down the hill to see if anyone was lurking around the neighborhood.

A young woman was sweeping the back stoop at the house of Amol Jindal, the new Indian pulp mill manager from Kenya. Two more women, far down the hill, were standing at an intersection holding hands and laughing. As she crossed Kwanza Street, she saw a woman wearing a brown and yellow *kanga* passing through the gate to Dr. Ogbo's house, but Anna couldn't see who she was. Nobody else was about. Anna shivered and returned to the house.

§§§

"Damn!" Aaron said when he came home for lunch. "We'll get to the bottom of this, I promise, even if we have to hire a guard. I won't have you frightened."

"I'm okay now," Anna said. "It was just a shock this morning. I've been thinking that if someone were really out to get us, they'd do something more aggressive, and we'd have an idea who it is."

"It could be any one of half a dozen people I've pissed off," he said. "It's the price of trying to do the right thing. Almost everyone who lives here deserves to have this mill running. Only a few see it as an opportunity to further their own interests."

"I don't want a guard," she said. "It would only segregate us further from the community."

He sighed. "You're right. And, I might add, you're damn brave. Still—" He paused, then looked at her sideways.

"A dog?" he asked.

"I'm pretty sure Simba believes she's canine," Anna said. "This morning she was sniffing the tail of our carved dog by the front door. Poor Simba. She sniffed and circled and sniffed again, meowed loudly and finally backed away, sulking, seeking the comfort of her food dish."

Aaron laughed, took Anna's hand and held it tight in his while becoming serious again. "Anna," he said, "I just made plans to meet with the Chief in Dar next week, and I expect to leave Monday morning. I know you're committed to the school on Wednesday. I'm not sure, now, that it would be a good idea to leave you here alone. Maybe Eva could handle the photography club?"

"This is Ahadi, not Baghdad," Anna said. "I'll be fine."

§§§

And she was fine, until Tuesday night, the second night Aaron was gone. At eleven, just beginning to doze off, she heard a rustling outside the patio door. She grabbed the flashlight beside the bed and padded her way to the sitting room, pulled back a corner of the curtain, peered outside and waited. A gecko slithered across the windowpane then disappeared. Wind whistled through the upper branches of the giant acacia tree in the corner of the yard. The wind died down. All was still.

Anna went back to bed, but, a few minutes later, she heard the sound again. This time she went to the sitting room and turned on the porch light. There was a quick flash of silver at the far left edge of the patio. She turned off the light. Simba jumped up on the window ledge beside her and stared out into the night. A minute passed. Anna turned the light on again and, this time, she saw a long bare leg disappear through the bougainvillea hedge. Simba yawned and jumped down from the ledge.

With Simba at her heels, Anna checked all the locks on the outside doors, brought the cat's bed, food and water dish into the bedroom and locked that door, too. Simba spent the night burrowed into Aaron's pillow, fast asleep. Anna dozed and woke, dozed and woke through the night.

She arose early enough to unlock the kitchen door for Tobias and check the perimeter of the house. There were no chickens or feathers in sight, nor any strange footprints; no droppings from birds or animals.

She moved Simba's bed and dishes back to the kitchen. "Did I imagine it?" she asked the cat.

Simba meowed and stared at the cupboard where her food was kept.

At times throughout the day, Anna remembered the flash of silver and bare legs, legs she had seen before. That night she doublechecked the doors, brought the cat into the bedroom and locked the door and slept the whole night without waking.

§§§

Joseph returned to school that afternoon and was the last student to come into the classroom for the photography club. He handed Anna the camera Eva had left at his house. "*Asante sana*," he said. Then, in English, "I like my picture."

It was all Anna could do to restrain herself from hugging him. "I'm glad you are here," she said. He grinned, lopsided, a dimple forming in his left cheek, then raced to his seat in the third row.

That day she had arranged for the children to go into the other classrooms and take pictures of their schoolmates learning new skills. "I want you to photograph your friends, but also to include what they are doing," she said. "It will be best if you focus on just one or two faces. Do you understand?"

The children nodded enthusiastically. "Wait until the moment is right. I don't want you to take more than five or six pictures the whole time you are there." She hoped they would learn to think about what they were seeing.

Anna showed them a few pictures she had developed: the boy riding his pony through the surf; the carver chiseling on a block of wood; the girl rolling a hoop through the narrow Street in Stonetown, Zanzibar. She asked Eva to explain to them how the relationship between the figure and the activity created a memorable image. Then she and Eva took them into the courtyard and directed them, two by two, to the cooking club, the music club, the art, horticulture and woodworking clubs. She avoided the far end of the schoolyard where boys were practicing with soccer balls.

When the children returned and handed in their cameras, they talked about what they had seen, and Eva translated. "I see Editha so happy to be singing," the oldest girl said. "The picture my cousin was painting looks exactly like a tree," Ashur said. Joseph spoke up in English. "My friend is making *twiga* grow from wood."

Anna smiled. The lesson seemed to have worked. She then handed them each a photocopy of a slip of paper which Eva had composed in Swahili. To spread out the number of children crowding into her small darkroom and to avoid any potential parental backlash, the slip of paper was to be signed by a parent. There were three boxes to check for days their child could attend the darkroom session and another box to check if the child could have a treat of chocolate cake and a "softi" drink such as Coca-Cola or Fanta Orange.

§§§

When the Land Cruiser pulled up to the house the next evening, Anna stepped outside to meet Aaron. She was surprised to see Daniel, rather than Jabari, driving.

"Daniel drove down with us to bring back a new Suzuki," Aaron explained. "It hadn't been serviced yet, so he was going to hang around another day to wait for it. But this morning, Daniel showed up at the hotel and told me Jabari wasn't feeling well—perhaps a bout of malaria. I wanted to get home to you, so we left a message with Jabari to pick up the Suzuki when he was better."

"You left him there?"

Aaron nodded. "He's with relatives and was in no shape to travel."

"At the Sip-Sip café?"

Again, Aaron nodded.

"I hope he's okay," Anna said. "Last week, remember, he said his stomach was upset and his hands were hurting."

"This morning it was chills and fever—very much like malaria," Aaron said. "He was going to get some medicine, so I'm sure we'll see him in a couple of days."

"Aaron, if Johani died of AIDS, you know the virus was probably transferred on birth. That means—"

"Unfortunately, what killed Johani remains a mystery. Still, we'll have Jabari checked out when he returns."

"By Doctor Ogbo?"

Aaron laughed. "Right, Ogbo would probably schedule Jabari for a hysterectomy."

§§§

The next Wednesday, the children were allowed to take their cameras home and complete the roll of film by photographing members of their family. After they were dismissed, Eva headed off to her new house on the corner of Tobias' lot.

Anna went to the head office. Grace Kampera was just locking the outside door.

"Where is your *piki-piki*?" Anna asked.

"No gas today," Grace said, "so she is having a small rest."

"I think I can find you some gas this evening," Anna said.

Grace smiled. "My *piki-piki* would be happy then."

"May I walk you home?" Anna asked.

"Ah, but I must go to the market," Grace replied.

"May I go with you?"

"Of course." They started off across the schoolyard.

"I think we have a big success with our after-school program," she said. "Just today a father of one of our students came to the school for the very first time to see his daughter singing in the chorus. And one mother reported that her son made very good pancakes at home."

"So, as you hoped, some parents are more interested in the school," Anna said. "And what about the volunteers?"

"They seem to like being teachers. Mahib Kamala—Hami's uncle—said the students are quick learners. He wants to plant a small garden at the end of the school yard and teach the children to tend it. He is going to ask you for some flowers to transplant."

"Wonderful!" Anna said. "I would like my garden to spread throughout the village. I'll also contribute a bucket for water and some small garden tools."

As they walked down the hill, Anna told Grace that she was concerned because, while every other student returned their permission slip to work in the darkroom, Joseph had not. When she asked him if he had the paper, Joseph just looked down at the floor, his little oval chin quivering as he shook his head.

"It is his father," she said. "I know it. And that Nigerian woman. Her name is Uwa."

"She is still here?"

"Yes, but Mama Joseph will not stand for it much longer. I think she will soon return from Dar with the two little girls, and that woman will be gone."

"Oh, the message was written in Kiswahili," Anna said. "Maybe Uwa wasn't able to read it. Could that be why it wasn't signed?"

"Maybe," Grace said. "But Joseph would have known that and given it to his father."

As they entered the market, Grace thrust out her arm to hold Anna back. "Look there," she whispered. "That is Uwa, the very same Nigerian woman."

Grace and Anna stood to the side, half hidden by a booth, as Uwa passed by. She was wearing a brown and yellow *kanga,* the same *kanga* Anna had seen the day the chicken was hanging from her front door. And her basket was overflowing with chickens, white chickens—at least four.

Grace trembled. "I didn't tell you," she said, "but Monday when I went to the school there was a chicken hanging from the doorknob of the office. It had no head. It's a—"

"Yes, I know," Anna said. "It's some kind of juju. A warning." She laughed. "We had the same, the Friday before and New Year's morning, as well. But now I think we know the source. Maybe we can get her deported."

CHAPTER THIRTY: ANOTHER WIFE

*I*ndeed, the next week, when Anna and Eva walked down to the school, they peered down Kwanza Street to see two young girls and a woman get into an Audi—not a company car. The woman was somewhat younger and slimmer than the Nigerian Mrs. Ogbu.

"I think Mama Joseph has returned," Anna said.

"I think that is a good thing," Eva said. "But I would not like that doctor for a husband."

"No, I wouldn't either," Anna said. "I think I am lucky to be married to Baba GM, and you are lucky to be married to Hami."

Eva smiled. "Mama, it is true," she said.

After class, Joseph came to the front of the room to speak to Anna. "I am sorry," he said. "I do not before give this paper to my father or his wife. But it is now here."

He reached deep into the pocket of his blue shorts and handed over the crumpled slip of paper. Each darkroom session was checked, as was permission for cake and a soft drink. The signature was unreadable and looked as if it had been forged by an eight-year old.

"Joseph, how did you learn to speak English so well?"

He smiled up at her, all front teeth present and gleaming, both cheeks dimpled. "My father's wife, she is teaching me." He hesitated, the smile disappearing, then added: "But she is now going away."

You mean, Mrs. Uwa Obgu from Nigeria? She knows English?"

Joseph backed away and turned his head. "No, Mama GM. That wife knows only something called Igala, I think. The wife, Layla, she work for Mr. McGowan and before that American. She learned even to read English." He faced Anna again, his voice rising with his enthusiasm. "When Baba not at our house, she even bring books—books with pictures and words—and tell me what they say."

Anna reeled with this new information. She motioned for Joseph to sit down on the bench in the front of the room and sat down beside him. "So your father has three wives? Uwa, his Nigerian wife, Mama Joseph, your mother, and also Layla?"

"Yes," he said, then paused for a minute. "Well, maybe."

"Joseph, I think you have signed this paper yourself. I am sure that you will very much enjoy learning how to print your pictures, but I need someone's okay before you can come to my house."

"I, myself, say okay."

When he looked at her, his eyes were bright and confident, his dimpled grin playful.

"You are an amazing kid," Anna said. "We'll work it out. I promise."

§§§

When Aaron arrived home, Anna had already poured herself some wine and had a tall glass of scotch waiting for him. She handed him the drink. "It's a nice evening," she said. "Let's go sit on the patio. I have a strange story to tell you."

"And I have disturbing news for you as well," he said.

They settled in at the table overlooking the garden.

"Okay, you first," Anna said.

Aaron took a sip of his scotch and leaned forward, his elbows resting on the glass tabletop.

"Okay. I found out today that Ryder McGowan and Jonas Shao had a disgusting deal going, where Shao would promise women some goods—perhaps charcoal or salt or fine cloth for a dress—or a raise, if the woman was in our employ. They would be asked to meet him at McGowan's house to receive the goods or discuss the raise."

Aaron swallowed, took a hefty gulp of his drink, then continued. "Once there, the payment was demanded—the payment being a roll in the hay. I understand that if the woman refused, she was not forced to have sex, though Shao made a few employees who refused so miserable they quit work. But a number of the women agreed. Some came back for more."

His face grew hard, and he gripped the edge of the table. "Now get this—if both Shao and McGowan were aroused, they flipped a coin to see who would win the honor of seducing the lady."

He shook his head, smiled sardonically. "At least, to my knowledge, they never formed a threesome."

"And Layla?"

"She's not saying. But the good news is that her father had a change of heart, and tonight he is to take the girl back to the tea plantation. With her knowledge of English, I expect she can find a good job there."

"That *is* good news about Layla. And, thank God, Shao and McGowan, those two scumbags, are gone," Anna said. "Can you find the women who refused and offer them their jobs back?"

"I'm already on that," he said. "In fact, Martha Wambura will start back at work in the morning, and I promoted her to financial manager. When she was Shao's assistant, she was doing most of his work anyway—at least the honest part."

He leaned back in the chair. "Unbelievable," he said. "Now it's your turn."

Anna told him of her conversation with Joseph.

"Wait a minute," Aaron said, shaking his head. "Layla, also his wife?"

"Well, like Joseph said, maybe. Maybe in a sense. Maybe not. Probably not legally. But it all fits. The Nigerian wife cast bad juju on us and the school to defend her husband as best as she could. And maybe Shao or McGowan impregnated Layla, but more likely Dr. Obgu himself. Remember Layla said the doctor only saw her at the clinic once and then was too busy? If he thought the child was his, he may have sent her packing."

"Didn't she first blame McGowan?" Aaron asked.

"That kind of makes sense, too," Anna said. "Maybe it was a way to get back at him. Or maybe it was McGowan who set her up with Ogbu in exchange for—"

"Yes. Medicine. I often wondered if his loopy behavior was attributed to alcohol, or if there was something else."

Anna took a sip of wine, sat back in her chair and continued. "Here's what I think. Layla is smart. She would have distrusted Shao and McGowan but had no choice but to do McGowan's bidding to keep her job. On the plus side, she won Joseph's affection when his mother was away."

"We'll probably never know the truth." Aaron paused, gazed out over the garden, then turned to her. "Say, you wouldn't happen to have another copy of that permission slip, would you?"

"I can make one," Anna said.

"Good. I'm going to pay the doctor a visit in the morning. And I promise you that the permission will be given."

Aaron got up and stood behind her, placed his hands on

her shoulders and kissed the top of her head. "Let's take a stroll through this spectacular garden, then have a bite to eat. And as soon as Jabari returns and the darkroom sessions are over, let's get the hell out of this crazy place. Let's head for the Serengeti. It's probably tamer."

As they walked down the last row of the vegetable garden, Anna reached up to pluck a mango from a tree. It felt ripe. She handed it to Aaron.

"I'm pretty sure the Garden of Eden was somewhere close by," he said. "But even if it was over near Kuwait, as some Biblical scholars claim, it had to have been a mango tree, not an apple tree, that God planted to test Adam and Eve."

"I'm looking forward to a little vacation from this garden of Eden," Anna said.

"I'm looking forward," Aaron said, "to getting away from the serpents. Though I think we are now down to just one."

They heard footsteps approaching on the dirt path adjacent to the garden and peered over the wall. "That's him," Anna whispered, "the man who never says a word."

The man looked up at them and waved his spear. "*Jambo*," he said, his voice raspy. He adjusted his loincloth and hurried on.

"Oh, he *does* talk," Anna whispered. "*Jambo*," she said back, her voice still hushed, then, just a little bit louder, "*Jambo!*" But the man didn't reply. Without looking back at them, he turned the corner, and all they could see was the back of his dusty, tangled hair heading down the hill.

"I think he was in the garden one night when you were gone," Anna said.

"Whoever he is, I think he's watching out for you."

Aaron put his arm around her waist. "Let's go inside and have another drink and then—I'm not really hungry. Are you?"

"Maybe we could just take a few bites of that mango and see what happens," Anna said.

"That's the best idea I've heard all week," Aaron said.

§§§

The next day, when Anna and Eva developed the students' rolls of film into negatives, Joseph's pictures again appeared to be best of them, especially the closeup profile of a boy leaning over a block of wood from which the rough head of an animal—possibly a giraffe—was just emerging. The photos he took at home were all pictures of his two sisters, the most imaginative one taken from the rear, a silhouette of them facing each other as they sat on the porch, sun setting over the valley in the distance.

Anna decided that the children, especially Joseph, needed to be inspired by the masters. When she couldn't get through to Christopher, she asked Aaron to telex the TV station where he worked. "Ask him if he'd ship out half a dozen of my photography books—including *Eudora Welty Photographs*, *The Family of Man* and *The World of Henri Cartier-Bresson*."

CHAPTER THIRTY-ONE:
POWERFUL MEDICINE

*A*nna tried daily, and finally reached Christopher by phone. She asked him if he wanted to fly to Arusha to join them for a safari through the Serengeti.

"Oh, Mom, that would be so cool, but I don't think it will work."

"Why not?"

"Well, first, there's the small matter of a passport, then I think I'd need a visa. And a few innoculations, and—"

"Christopher, you had the passport form ready to mail before we left."

"I kind of forgot to put it in the envelope. And, well—I have a dentist appointment."

"That could be changed—if you had a passport."

"Not exactly."

"Christopher? What's going on?"

"Well, do you remember that wisdom tooth they didn't remove when I was nineteen? It's been acting up a bit, so it may have to come out. I have an appointment with the oral surgeon on June sixth.

"Why do you have to wait so long?"

"Um, well, I think they want to see first if the antibiotics work."

"You're on antibiotics? Christopher, how long has this been going on?"

"It's okay, Mom, really. Just a small thing."

"Is it impacted?"

"No, it's broken through, Mom. They won't have to dig it out much."

"How much?"

"A little much."

"Still, someone should be with you."

"Mom, it's just a small, unnecessary tooth. Beryl is going to drive me to the dentist and—"

"Oh, Honey. Have you and Beryl made up?"

"Yep. A couple of weeks ago."

"That's wonderful news. I'm so glad," she said.

"Me, too," he said.

Still, Anna was worried. A tooth extraction. Okay, *only* a tooth extraction. Not a big deal. And, after all, Christopher was now a grown man. But he was also still her child. Her only child.

"Christopher, are you telling me the whole truth?"

"Scout's honor, Mom. I'm fine. In fact, the other reason I can't come is that I have an interview at WGBH in Boston on the tenth of June. They want to talk to me about a job. They're the best. It could be a huge promotion, starting in September. But maybe I could start later, if you still need me to stay here."

"No. We'd work that out. Have you given up on graduate school?"

"I'm actually working on that, too. I've almost finished my applications for NYU and Columbia and going to check out BU while I'm in Boston."

"Does your boss know you're considering another job?"

"He recommended me and told me to put in for some vacation time to go down for the interview. He said if I didn't want to move, I still had a job in Vermont. And, Mom, you don't have to worry. While I'm gone overnight, Beryl is staying at the house with Murray. She graduates on the weekend. Is it okay if her parents stay here?"

"Of course."

"That's good, because I already invited them."

"Oh, how I wish I could be there! Will you get Beryl a graduation gift from Dad and me? Maybe a Gary Milek landscape print? Does she have a job lined up? You *will* make sure the house is clean, won't you?"

Christopher laughed. "You're beginning to sound like my mother. Beryl's staying on at the Dartmouth Bookstore for the summer while she looks for a job in publishing. Maybe Boston or New York. The print sounds like a great gift. Also, the weekend after this, the Rothchilds invited us up to their cabin on Holland Pond in the Northeast Kingdom. We're taking the canoe—and Murray. They even promised us a lobster dinner!"

Anna breathed deeply, caught up in his enthusiasm and sorting through all he had told her—toothache, Beryl, her parents, WBGH, grad school, Boston, New York, Holland Pond, lobster dinner. "Okay, Sweetheart. But, if you can get through by phone or telex, let me know how the extraction goes. And the job interview. And enjoy these special times."

"I will, Mom. Say hi to Dad."

"I love you, Christopher."

For once, the phone didn't go dead before Christopher had a chance to say, "I love you, too. We'll talk again soon."

When the conversation ended, she started to hang up the handset, but it was as if, to do so, she would lose her son.

Anna had no idea how telephones transmitted across continents and oceans, but she knew her connection to Christopher had nothing to do with cables and wires. It had to do with a tenderness which had matured, year by year, just as they had both matured. She finally replaced the handset on the receiver and walked out the patio door.

She studied the profusion of color edging the garden and, beyond, the scarp of the vast fertile valley, a vista that she had come to treasure every bit as much as she treasured the view of the river from their deck in Vermont.

To the left, a thin wisp of smoke ascended from the mill. She smiled and returned to the house, confident that she and Aaron—and Christopher, too—were exactly where they were meant to be.

That night, over dinner, Anna told Aaron what Christopher had said. "He'll be fine with that tooth," Aaron said. "It should have come out with the others when he was nineteen."

"I hope it will be okay," Anna said. "And, oh, I realize that you have reservations, but Beryl's back in his life. In fact, she's graduating this weekend, and—"

"Good. I like Beryl."

"But you said—"

Aaron cocked his head and looked over at Anna, his expression asking her for forgiveness. "I know. That was a dumb thing to say. I just want for Christopher to be happy. Actually, I think she'd be a terrific mother for our grandchildren."

"Grandchildren! Yikes! I have way too much to do before I start to worry over grandchildren."

"Me, too," Aaron said. "Let's hope they hold off a while."

§§§

The next morning, Jabari was waiting at the front door, having finally returned from Dar. Anna followed Aaron out to the driveway. "I left the new Suzuki down at the motor pool," Jabari said. "The gear shift isn't punching back at me like the old ones, but the ride is still bump-a, bump-a."

Anna looked him over. "Are you all well now?"

"Yes, Mama. The doctor in Dar gave me powerful medicine, and the fever is all gone."

Anna expected Aaron to tell Jabari to have a complete checkup, but, instead, he said, "That's great! Do you feel like driving to Arusha week after next? We plan to visit the Serengeti."

Jabari grinned. "I hope, sir, we are taking the Land Cruiser, not the Suzuki."

"Absolutely," Aaron said. "Anna, do you need a driver for anything today?"

She shook her head, still examining Jabari closely. Indeed, his skin tone was normal and his eyes clear. He seemed to have lost a few pounds, but that would have been expected after a bout of malaria. Still, she was concerned.

"What did the doctor say was the problem, Jabari?"

"Some malaria, Mama. I have now finished the pink pills. And the doctor gave me a powerful protector." He raised the right leg of his khaki pants. Circling a white sock was a loose string of yellow beads.

Anna knew that asking him to see Doctor Ogbu would be a waste of time. And she figured he'd have to be admitted to the hospital in Iringa to get an exam. But there was one option available.

"Before we leave for Arusha," she said, "will you let Babu Bungara check you over? He might have an even more powerful charm."

Almost immediately, she regretted asking, thinking she might have slighted Aaron and offended Jabari. And what was she thinking, sending him to a medicine man? But she trusted Bungara to, at least, check him over as best as he could.

Both men looked at each other and nodded. "Yes, Mama. That is a good idea," Jabari said. Then he smiled. "I think there are many *simbas* in the Serengeti, and I will want to carry powerful medicine."

Anna laughed.

"Okay, Jabari," Aaron said. "If Mama GM doesn't need you today, let's get to the mill. Then you can take the car down to see Babu Bungara and come back to pick me up."

Jabari and Aaron hopped in the Land Cruiser and sped out of the driveway.

When they returned that afternoon, Jabari said that Babu Bungara had declared him fit to travel. He had wrapped around his ankle, above the yellow beads, a band of square purple beads, one larger, round and silver, emblazoned with the face of a *simba*. He also gave him a vial of pills to take, just in case. To Anna, they looked like amoxicillin.

§§§

Three times in the coming week, four shy and nervous children arrived at the house. They chose two pictures to print, watched in astonishment as their negatives became images, laughed as they ran out to the patio for a slice of Tobias' chocolate cake, enthusiastically said, "*Asante Sana,* Mama GM," as they left the house, racing each other down the hill, carrying their photographs home.

There was a final meeting of the photography club before the month-long break in June. As much as Anna wanted to give the children the cameras they had been using, she knew that obtaining film and developing pictures would be a problem for them. Instead, she loaded each camera and told the children to take all the pictures they wanted of the primary school celebration, a special event Grace Kampera designed to honor the new skills the children had learned

260

in the after-school program. Volunteers and parents were invited. Non-essential mill employees were given two hours off work.

And the schoolyard was packed. There was singing and dancing, and a table heaped with soft drinks the school board had contributed and cookies Tobias and his students had made the day before in Anna's kitchen. Benches were brought out from the classrooms to display the children's accomplishments: photographs, paintings, wood carvings, even a small hand-crafted wooden table, a model bridge, a logo and typed by-laws for *Baraza la Wanafunz*, the new student council. Excited children led their parents to benches displaying their work: landscape drawings, potted plants, stories written out by hand in English and bound by paper clips. The track team raced around the perimeter of the schoolyard, and the football club held a short, choreographed exhibition, passing the ball to the beat of a drum from player to player, foot to head to foot to head.

The joyous afternoon of celebration ended with a final song from the music club, the Tanzanian anthem. "*Tubariki watoto wa Africa.*" Anna bowed her head and dabbed at tears formed by pride, by wonder, and by sorrow, knowing that today would be a pinnacle from which too many of these children would descend. She whispered, "Bless us, children. Bless us all."

A Tanzanian Story

CHAPTER THIRTY-TWO:
A CHILD OF AFRICA

*T*hey left early Saturday and drove due north, then east, stopping the next day at Tarangire to watch baboons grooming each other. At Lake Manyara, they paused beneath a leopard, high in a tree, mouth red with blood, and the remains of a dik dik clenched between his legs. They descended with a guide into Ngorongoro Crater, the 3-million-year-old inactive volcanic caldera, 2000 feet deep and ranging over 100 square miles, deep enough to trap elephants, wildebeest, giraffes and rhinos. A white rhino appeared with her baby in tow. They moved in as close as they could. Anna kept the motor drive going. *Whir, whir, whir.*

With each day, Aaron seemed more engaged with the landscape, the array of wonders spread out before them. Anna began to realize how much tension he was releasing. He joked. He laughed. He took her gently in his arms each night and slept peacefully through the next dawn.

They entered the plains of the Serengeti to vast vistas of grasslands dotted by ponds, kopjes, broad acacia trees. They spotted bush pigs, cheetah, elands, gazelles, hippos, oryx, antelopes, wart hogs, zebras. Even a tiny bat eared fox.

"No mosquitoes will bother us today," Jabari said with a grin.

They followed a family of lions down a narrow dirt road, then stopped to photograph a lion king atop a kopje, scanning his realm. The lion's eyes narrowed. *Click. Click.* He rose on his haunches and opened his mouth wide, as if to roar. His four canine teeth were huge. *Click, click, click.* Jabari never flinched.

The lion yawned and settled back down. Jabari chuckled and drove on.

They stayed overnight at the Lobo Wildlife Lodge, a stone and timber structure built into a rocky outcrop. From their second-floor room, they could view the plains, a kopje in the distance, herds of zebra and clusters of wildebeest just beginning their annual migration.

When Jabari left to fill the Land Cruiser with petrol, Anna and Aaron went to the lobby to use the hotel phone to call Christopher. The tooth was extracted, no problem, the job offer not all he expected. Beryl's graduation was great. The house was clean. He caught two bass on a flyrod at Holland Pond. He was a happy young man.

§§§

Though they'd only been gone a week, it was time to head south to Ahadi. Anna ached for Aaron as he kept looking out the window of their room while stuffing his bag with dirty socks and shirts. She wished for him a longer time away from the mill, from the problems he so readily shouldered.

They took one last detour down a rough road, largely uninhabited except for occasional clusters of Maasai goat herders. Finally, they reached Olduvai Gorge, the vast, steep-sided ravine carved into the Eastern Serengeti Plains by a succession of ancient rivers. Here, in 1959, paleontologists Mary and Louis Leakey unearthed a *Homo habilis* skull, an inhabitant of this dry riverbed some two million years ago—perhaps the remains of the first human species.

They toured the museum, with Jabari pausing at every skull, every drawing of ancient people and extinct animals.

Outside, Anna watched the two of them, Aaron and

Jabari, examine fossils and skulls. They ran their fingers through volcanic ash and inspected the assortment of shapes materializing in their hands. Slowly Jabari, then Aaron, walked down a long, corrugated slab of volcanic rock. They knelt to examine the slab closely, discussing the possible secrets it held.

A few minutes passed, then they looked up at each other, and their eyes locked for a long moment. Anna photographed them as they seemed to recognize, as Anna recognized, more profoundly than ever before, their shared heritage, common birthright.

The three of them walked in silence toward the Land Cruiser, as if language could not express what they felt, and, two kilometers away, they made one last stop at a crescent-shaped dune. There, billions of grains of black ash continuously flowed in cadence, rolling, shimmering, refusing to settle. Aaron grabbed a handful of sand and tossed it in the air. But instead of the wind blowing it away, the grains clumped together into black iron filings and fell straight to earth.

Anna stood beside her husband and looked toward the distant mountains, imagining herself transported some four million years into the past. East African apes were just beginning to walk on two legs. Two million years later, those apes had evolved to make stone tools. She thought of human brains developing the capacity to speak, then to create art, to envision and establish civilizations, each nation growing more distinct due to the available raw materials and natural environment. She wondered when her own ancestors might have migrated out of the Great Rift Valley, and where they might have gone.

And, at this moment, Anna realized that, despite the

many generations that separated her from this land, despite subsequent tongues, religions, traditions and variations in skin color, she remained a child of Africa. Like the grains of shifting sand surrounding them, she and Africa were both separate and inevitably bound together.

PART FIVE

Kwaheri
Goodbye
July through September, 1991

CHAPTER THIRTY-THREE: SORROW

*A*nna feared that Jabari would die. She'd feared it since the day she followed him into the Sip Sip Café. She believed it when she saw him sitting on the curb of the hospital, the purple yarn of Johani's doll protruding from the top of a paper sack. She knew he was starting to die when he complained that his head ached, his hands hurt; when it took him weeks to fight off a bout of malaria.

She guessed he would begin to lose weight, and he did. She guessed he would scratch at a rash, which he did. He would become too weak to drive, then too weak to move. Within a month, Jabari couldn't rise from the pallet on which he lay. He writhed in agony. He needed morphine, and plenty of it, morphine which Doctor Ogbu said he didn't have.

It might have been fate, that night in July, when Doctor Ogbu left the Bwana Club, having downed, it was said, half a bottle of vodka, and tripped six feet from his car. It might have been fate, but nobody could account for the wound in his gut—ragged at the edges like the shape of a spear.

The bartender sent the dishwasher off to find Daniel,

the driver. They loaded Ogbu into the back seat of Ogbu's car, and Daniel hightailed it to the hospital in Iringa. Daniel returned bringing a set of keys to Rebecca, the nurse, who unlocked the clinic's secret storage room and went to Jabari's house with a syringe and vial of morphine.

Ogbu survived. Jabari slept peacefully through his last two days.

CHAPTER THIRTY-FOUR: CONTEMPLATION

*J*abari died just after sunset. One of his twins knocked on the door, tears streaming down his face. Anna held him, then she and Aaron drove him home. Dafina, Jabari's wife, stood outside her house, her face composed, her arm around the other twin. Anna clasped her hand. "Oh, *Pole sana*," Anna said. "*Siku ya huzuni*, such a sad day."

Dafina nodded. "*Asante sana*." She let out a deep breath and opened the front door. Aaron went inside, but Anna couldn't bear to enter. With Jabari, they'd crisscrossed the country for a year and a half. He'd seen them through storms, bargained for treasures, faced down his fears and mourned the death of his child. Anna wanted to remember him alive, laughing, contemplating, his eyes locked on Aaron's, a brother from long ago.

She walked back to the car to wait for Aaron, sat on the running board, her head raised toward the stars, the Southern Cross now a remembrance, Orion bright, a full moon rising, hazy through her tears.

Aaron got into the driver's seat where Jabari had sat for so many miles. He patted the wheel before turning the key and shifting into reverse, but didn't apply the gas. Instead, he looked back at the house. "Jabari was holding the amulet, the one with the silver *simba*. He was at peace."

Aaron shook his head. "The carpenter has the box ready. I'll drop you at home, then run down to Daniel's house to tell him to use the pickup to take Jabari and the family to his mother's village."

At home, Anna rummaged through the pile of pictures she had printed. She selected three to give to Dafina. In one picture, Jabari was grinning at Aaron, a pair of baboons grinning behind them. In another, he was looking closely at the rabbit mask. The third was a profile of Jabari at the wheel of the car in the Serengeti, a lion seated on a kopje just beyond.

She'd reprint these pictures for herself and Aaron, pictures that would always remind them of an extraordinary time when they knew a man strong enough, brave enough to say he was afraid of lions.

CHAPTER THIRTY-FIVE: HOPE

$\mathcal{A}$nna studied the picture she had taken of Jabari and Aaron in Olduvai Gorge. Their faces radiated profound respect for each other. She was certain that this was the moment they both recognized their brotherhood.

Scrubland surrounded the dry lakebed where they were standing, and, on the horizon, a mountain range levitated over the haze. She looked at the picture and felt an extraordinary sense of serenity. It was as if she had captured the true spirit of Africa—in the gentle faces of Jabari and Aaron, yes—but, more so, because of the vast, quiet landscape in which they stood. This spirit, she believed, had nurtured humans from their beginnings and would endure long after the colonists and missionaries and capitalists gave up trying to cast Africa into something she was never meant to be.

§§§

When Aaron came through the door, Simba rubbed up against him. He picked her up, then sat on the loveseat, stroking her while she calmly purred. Anna sat down beside them. For a few minutes, they were silent, then began to reminisce, back and forth about Jabari.

"Do you remember when he bargained for a photograph with the Maasai?"

"That first night in Mikumi?"

"The picture he drew of the Land Cruiser?"

"Outside the hospital the day Johani died?"

"How we cried together?"

"How we laughed!"

271

"How quickly Simba took to him!"

They were, again, silent for a while, each absorbed by their own memories, then Aaron asked, "How do you think Simba would take to snow?"

"She'd probably do fine, but you know what Murray thinks of cats," Anna said. "And Eva has told me she'd take care of Simba when we leave."

"If they want to adopt Simba, they'd need more than a length of cloth for an outside door," Aaron said.

"We could arrange for a real door. Or a job and a house for them, if not here, maybe at the tea plantation. Hami's English has really improved, and he'll obtain his GED before long. Eva could finish secondary school. She'd make a fine teacher. And I think Tobias might be ready to start his bakery."

She reached over and caressed the scruff of fur between Simba's ears. "What I'd really like to take back home is a kid named Joseph."

"I'm with you there," Aaron said. He settled deeper into the cushion and turned his head toward her. "I'm afraid, though, that his mother might object."

"Unfortunately, I think you have a point." She leaned closer to Aaron, and Simba turned around and lay her head in Anna's lap.

"Aaron," she said, running her hand down Simba's back, "are you saying that we're going home soon?"

Aaron nodded. "I think I've done all I can do here, and we should be able to get everything squared away by September. The Indians have the mill under control, and I heard today from Howard Hammond that the Vermont mill is down for the third time in a month. I think he was hinting that I might want to try to rescue it again."

"So, if we leave, we can stay in Vermont?"
"I wouldn't have it any other way, would you?"

§§§

They obtained new jobs for Hami and Eva at the tea plantation and staked Tobias' bakery. They gave away their clothes and food, books, cameras and film, and packed up their masks, sculptures, baskets, negatives and photographs.

The school staged a celebration for Anna. They dressed her in a *kanga*, and the children danced and sang to her in English.

> *"Bye-bye, our mother. Safe Journey.*
> *Our Mother, thank you.*
> *Although you will go far away,*
> *We will never forget you. "*

She stood before the assembled children, a sea of white shirts and blue shorts and skirts, knowing she was being given back more—so much more—than she deserved. In the crowd of children, she sought out Joseph and Jabari's boys, and shy little Busara who understood that you can love someone when you try very hard to know them.

She then looked at Grace Kampera, standing to her right, and Marianna Mongo, on her left, at Aaron, close behind, between Hami and Tobias. She missed Jabari intensely, but there was his wife, Dafina. Eva was holding onto Dafina's arm.

Anna looked at each of them, then faced the children and said, "*Nakupenda nyote.* I love you all."

§§§

Early the next morning, Daniel arrived in the Land Cruiser, and they slipped away from the house without being noticed. They drove down the hillside, past the dispensary, the empty tennis court, the school, the sprawling mill, smoke billowing from each of the tall stacks. They passed the market, and, just before they reached the gate, a tall man wearing only a loincloth and carrying a spear waved them down. Daniel slowed, and Anna leaned forward from the back seat, telling him to stop.

"But this man, he never speaks," Daniel said.

"Oh, I think he will," Anna said.

She rolled down her window, and the man approached within a few yards of the car. "*Kwaheri,*" he said, his voice mellow. "*Safari Njema.*"

Daniel turned, astonished, to look back at Anna. "Oh, he speaks! He says good-bye and have a safe trip."

"I want to thank him." Anna said. "*Asante. Asante sana.*"

The man smiled, nodded and turned, quickly disappearing down a narrow dirt path into the woods. They watched him vanish, then continued through the gate, leaving Ahadi, the town called Promise, where, for a short time, Anna Chadwick belonged to a village she learned to call her home.

CODA

I once lived in a Tanzanian village which rose from a desolate valley reached by a long, unpaved road—a village built to house workers in a government-owned paper mill. While Ahadi, the village of this novel, houses mill workers and bears a similarity in locale and design, it is not the town where I lived.

I knew Muslims and Christians and animists: gardeners, cooks, drivers, children, market vendors, shopkeepers, missionaries, mill workers, a dedicated headmistress and men who hunted with spears. I knew expatriates—most compassionate, some arrogant and some determined to replace established values with their own. But the characters depicted in *Like a Mask Dancing* are fictional.

Even Simba, the cat in this novel, is not the very same Simba we fed each morning and night. Nor am I Anna, the woman who tells this story. Only the character Aaron resembles—though not exactly—the man with a dream, with an adventurous spirit and heavy briefcase I twice followed to Africa.

Yet the various sections of the city of Dar Es Salaam, the Serengeti, the dramatic rural landscapes are described as I remember them. The vibrant birds and grand beasts, rivers snaking through canyons, the vast plains and deep gorges, rich grass and rolling hills are, as Alan Paton describes in *Cry, the Beloved Country*: "lovely beyond any singing of it."

In *Summertime*, South African novelist J. M Coetzee drew from Franz Kafka, saying: "A book should be an axe to chop open the frozen sea inside us." I wrote this book to dive into the sea of my extraordinary experiences in Africa, to revisit all I left behind; to ask forgiveness for all I left undone. — *Sally Stiles*

END NOTES

$\mathcal{T}$racking data for Tanzania between 1990 and 2017, the Institute for Health Metrics and Evaluation, based at the University of Washington in Seattle, reports on their website that the population of Tanzania in 2017 reached 54 million people with an average of 5.6 years of education. Per capita GDP was $2,685 (compared to the 2017 USA per capita GDP of $59,484.)

In these 27 years, there have been improvements in observed life expectancy which increased by nearly twelve years for women and just over ten years for men. In 2017, women were expected to live to an average of 65.8 years and men to an average of 62.1. During the same period, deaths per 1,000 live births decreased from 98.9 to 43.3 for children under the age of one. (Still, consider that the same infant mortality rate in the USA in 2017 was 5.7.)

In 2007, HIV/AIDS was the leading cause of death. By 2017, with unsafe sex decreasing 70.8% as a risk factor (and better identification and treatment methods), deaths due to HIV/AIDS decreased by 75.3 percent and dropped to third place. Neonatal disorders and lower respiratory infections moved up to first and second place. Tuberculosis remained the fifth largest cause of death. After ten years, malaria contributed to 13.7% fewer fatalities. Heart disease and diabetes, leading causes of death in developed countries, began to rise.

Between 1990 and 2017, the index for healthcare access and quality improved from 21.9 to 33.9. (The index for the United States is 86.3.)

healthdata.org/Tanzania

*I*n 1993, Ted Conover wrote an article for The New Yorker entitled "Trucking through the AIDS Belt," about the role of long-distance drivers in spreading HIV across the African continent.

According to the Farlex Free Dictionary, "AIDS belt is a term used early in the AIDS epidemic, which referred to tropical African nations with more than 1,000 cases of AIDS, where AIDS affected heterosexuals and was linked to increased sexual activity; the 'belt' countries were: Burundi, Central African Republic, Kenya, Malawi, Rwanda, Tanzania, Uganda, Zaire, and Zambia."

A portion of sales will be donated to rural Africa's Community Health Partners, specifically for their HIV/AIDS Care & Treatment Program which provides HIV testing & counseling, palliative care, antiretroviral therapy, TB treatment, and prevention of Mother to Child Transmission. *https://chp.or.ke*

A Tanzanian Story

ACKNOWLEGEMENTS

*I*t takes a village to write a book.

I am grateful to so many people who saw me through *Like a Mask Dancing*. There were days, actually months, when it appeared that Anna and Aaron would never appear on a printed page. But they did appear—with thanks to the encouragement of my publisher, Pale Horse Books, and my stellar writing group: John Conlee, Kathleen Jabs, James Tobin, Greg Lilly and Lee Alexander.

A year before publication, Jim Tobin wrote: "I hope you don't give up on Anna. I, for one, want to follow her to the end of her journey."

Phyllis Barber, once again, urged me deeper into the clay, which, though messy at times, was ultimately rewarding.

Even in a work of fiction, the historical facts must be accurate. Anania Mpotwa, Carol Shaben and Dr. Carrie Dolan graciously lent me their expertise.

Writers Dalia Pagani, Patricia Gray, Katheryn Lovell and Dr. Donna Davenport provided essential suggestions and support, as did astute readers Susan Baer, Jennie Capps, Pat Luke, Shelley Roeder, Joan Seamon, Carolyn Smith, Joeann Jacoby, Janis Walby and Amanda Wareing.

And I continue to be grateful to the many African authors who inspire me. — *Sally Stiles*

A Tanzanian Story

PRE-PUBLICATION COMMENTS:

"Very moving and effective."
—Professor John Conlee

"Thoroughly enjoyable!"
—Janis Walby

"A fascinating journey."
—Joeann Jacoby

"I keep rewinding the book in my mind,
picture by picture."
—Susan Baer

"I really loved this book!"
—Katheryn Lovell

"Interesting, eye-opening, sad, romantic
and full of love and compassion.
Sally Stiles has written another great book!"
—Shelley Roeder

"What an adventure!"
—Jennie Capps

"BRAVO!"
—Amanda Wareing

"Moving, thoughtful, nuanced, full of passion and insight."
—Carol Shaben

<<<<◇>>>>

CPSIA information can be obtained
at www.ICGtesting.com
Printed in the USA
FSHW011153121020
74639FS